CW00631389

# Great Britain
# Little England

## Who's fooling whom?

Richard Hill

A Division of Europublic SA/NV

Published by Europublications, Division of Europublic SA/NV,
Avenue Winston Churchill 11 (box 21), B-1180 Brussels.
Tel: + 32 2 343 77 26, Fax: + 32 2 343 93 30.

*Cover design: Taouffik Semmad with the assistance of Karim Guendouzi*

Cartoons reproduced by permission of Punch.

Printed in Belgium. Edition et Imprimerie, Brussels.
D/1994/6421/3                                    ISBN 90-74440-04-5

*For Audrey and Leslie who made me English,*
*even if they disagree with a lot of what I say.*

# Contents

I remember thinking, when the Hand of Providence swept me over to the Continent nearly 30 years ago, that the best thing anyone could do with the Dear Old Country (DOC) was tow it across to the Caribbean and turn it into a banana republic. It seemed the best solution for a nation so clearly dedicated to muddle and incompetence.

Today this solution doesn't make sense. For a start, the DOC is umbilically and irrevocably committed to the Continent by the Channel Tunnel. So it has to stay where and what it is – part of Europe – even if its inhabitants keep on calling me up and asking me 'what's the weather like in Europe?' (maybe because TV meteorologists keep on talking about 'the weather over in Europe').

But I can offer another solution to the DOC dilemma, one that occurred to me when an American journalist in Paris asked me what I thought about EuroDisney and I preferred to change the subject. Since there is now this new and hopefully efficient direct link with the island, instead of towing the country across to the Caribbean, why not leave it where it is and turn it into a theme park? For the problem today is no longer one of simple muddle and incompetence, it is a paralysing attachment to nostalgia, symbolism, sentimentality and, frankly, myth. Of course, this attachment was always there, it's just that much more evident today.

Turn the country into a theme park, and the British – and particularly the English – will be able to go on pursuing their unique way of life, and foreigners will be able to savour it for a flat fee levied at the Channel Tunnel entrance-exit.

The Chancellor of the Exchequer will then be able to restore the locals' faith in the political establishment by giving them money instead of taking it away from them – and the locals will be able to indulge their quality of life without bothering about silly things like progress.

Now you may think that, even if I'm joking, I have something serious on my chest. 'Actually', as some people still say in England, you're right: thirty years of watching things go wrong when they shouldn't. And I intend to get them off my chest.

I will cover familiar ground, maybe a number of times, in the course of these pages: put that down to subjectivity and my sense of involvement. But I am not going to offer a closely documented indictment of the manner in which this country is run, which has already been done by people with far better credentials. I'm more concerned about the mindsets, motivations, mannerisms – and, inevitably, character flaws – of the people involved, the English.

There is so much talent and promise locked up in this little island that failure to exploit it ranks as little less than a crime against humanity – both against the birthright of the English, and against the right of foreigners to enjoy what the English could bring to life if only their system gave them the chance. But the odds are against this, as long as their present state of mind and the present manner of governance persist.

Incidentally, if anyone thinks I am arguing for closer adhesion to the European Union or am about to invoke the 'F' word, they are wrong. That has nothing whatever to do with the book.

What does have to do with this book is the unwitting inspiration of many thousands of my fellow-countrymen and women. I also have a debt of gratitude to those who offered their encouragement and comments during the preparation of these pages, in particular Frances De Handschutter, Jason Hadick, Eric Leach, Chris Leeds of the Université de Nancy II, Nigel Tutt and Nick Winkfield.

*"From this amphibious ill-born mob began*
*That vain, ill-natured thing, an Englishman"*

**Daniel Defoe, *The True-Born Englishman***

*"A young Scotsman of your ability let loose upon the world*
*with £300, what could he not do? It's almost appalling to*
*think of; especially if he went among the English."*

**Sir James Barrie, *What Every Woman Knows***

*"But Lord! to see the absurd nature of Englishmen, that can-*
*not forbear laughing and jeering at everything that looks*
*strange."* **Samuel Pepys, *Diary*, 27/11/1662**

*"What happens outside Great Britain does not greatly interest*
*the public at large, except on occasions when the Government*
*is given an opportunity to silence those foreigners who have*
*the presumption to place their own interests before those of the*
*British."* **Philippe Daudy, *Les Anglais: Portrait of a People***

*"...as western peoples go, the English are very highly*
*differentiated."* **George Orwell, *The Lion and the Unicorn***

*"This week a mongrel race with delusions of homogeneity, a*
*superiority complex and a chip on its shoulder is set to make*
*a monumental show of indifference to relations with its*
*neighbours while indulging in an orgy of nostalgia for old*
*battles."* **Peter Millar, *The Sunday Times*, 5/6/1994**

*"The English, rather than having a dual identity like the*
*Welsh and Scots, tend to possess a fused identity, best*
*described as Anglo-British. Further, this identity has been*
*said to be strongly associated with the rulers rather than*
*with the people below. This observation reinforces a view or*
*theory that the traits of past aristocratic rulers have helped*
*to form the norms in England."* **Sir Christopher Leeds, Bt.**

*"Living in England, provincial England, must be like*
*being married to a stupid but exquisitely beautiful wife."*
**Margaret Halsey, *With Malice Toward Some***

# Great Britain
# Little England

From the title of this book, you will gather that I am making a play of 'Great' and 'Little', and also of 'Britain' and 'England'. The term 'Little Englanders' was, I understand, first applied to those who questioned the country's imperial ambitions. Today the wheel has turned full circle.

In my view the distinction between 'Britain' and 'England' – and by inference between the British and the English – is more important than the counterpoint between 'Great' and 'Little'.

There is of course a lot of overlap between the British and the English, though the concept of 'Britishness' is too complex culturally to even rate as a definition. Some people maintain it only had real meaning for the time that the nation had an empire. But in some essentials the differences between the English and their island cohabitants are marked – and not just genetically.

The English share, in varying degrees, the virtues of creativity, wit and decency with their fellows in the British Isles, Celtic and others. But they rarely pass their vices on to them, despite the presence of laminae of English culture in the Celtic fringe, like the 'English Scots' who stand out from the 'Scots Scots' like perfumed roses in a patch of thistles, and the anglicised aristocracy of Ireland (parenthetically it is curious how the Celts, or the Continentals come to that, when they do get assimilated into the English culture, tend to end up even more tribalised than the home-grown variety!).

These English vices are well enough known to the English, but we tend to forget or overlook them, or pretend they are not there. They include excessive sentimentality, nostalgia, humbug extending to hypocrisy, occasional pomposity and snobbishness (both the conventional and the inverted varieties) and an accumulation of organically grown or assumed values which no longer relate to reality and make absolutely no sense to any self-respecting foreigner.

Most of these vices have received short shrift with our neighbours in the British Isles. For one thing they have their own: dourness and even duplicity in some cases, rabid sectarianism in others. But at least they know what they're like, warts and all, whereas we English still don't seem to know, or want to know, what makes us different from the rest – the rest being all those other Europeans who know what they are up to and, quite cynically, just go on doing it.

Being straightforward is a particularly Scottish thing, something that tends to set these people apart from the other inhabitants of the British Isles, the folk of Northern England excluded. It is remarkable how many of the most plain-spoken and effective members of the Lower House are Scots.

*'It's no good – I just can't seem to think of myself as a European yob'.*

A *Eurobarometer* study [1] conducted for the European Commission in late-1993 stumbled on another very essential difference between the English and the British. UK citizens were asked whether they felt 'British' and 'European' at one and the same time. Only 37% of the UK sample felt European in any way: 59% felt British only. But, as a footnote in the study points out, rather ungrammatically, "Scottish and Welsh are significantly more often 'also European' as compared to the English."

With the English feeling themselves to be different from, and by implication superior to, their neighbours both within and outside the British Isles, it is hardly surprising that it is the Englishness of the island community that stands out most starkly in contrast to European cultures generally. Pierre Daninos was doing more than just perpetuating a stereotype when he took the character of Major Thompson for the book he wrote back in the 50s – even if this stereotype seems a bit far-fetched today [2].

It is curious that, although they are well enough aware of the differences, most Continentals can't be bothered to make the distinction between the English and the British. This is even true of the French, despite their centuries-old rivalry with the English and their *belle alliance* with the Scots, with whom they exchanged naturalisation privileges in 1513. An example is the title of Philippe Daudy's book, referred to a number of times in these pages [3]: '*Les Anglais*: Portrait of a People', not '*Les Britanniques*'...

Of course, as George Mikes pointed out in *How to be an Alien* [4], there is little advantage for a Continental in knowing the difference: "A foreigner cannot improve. Once a foreigner, always a foreigner. There is no way out for him. He may become British; he can never become English." Unless he happens to be a Jamaican who is good at cricket, as a perceptive friend of mine who knows more about these things than I do said.

17

But there is another important difference between the English and the rest that does impinge on the consciousness of impressionable foreigners: English fans riot at football matches, non-English British fans don't. Although a great unifier (all Europeans love association football), the game has become one of the most significant expressions of cultural differences – it may be the best evidence I have that such differences exist.

Finally, setting aside these cultural nuances, there is another counterpoint between 'Great Britain' and 'Little England', the difference between the formal (even more formally, 'the United Kingdom of Great Britain and Northern Ireland') and the intimate.

To me, the intimate seems much closer to the reality.

*"The English can never be convinced by arguments, only by facts."*
**Attributed to Jean Monnet**

*"Every so often something comes along to remind us that English phlegm has also cost this nation dear. A wilful blindness to the true dimensions of a problem has all too often prevented a sufficiently speedy or vigourous response."*
**John Harper, *The Guardian*, 18/6/1987**

*"An Englishman's mind works best when it is almost too late."*
**Lord D'Abernon**

*"Lumping all other European countries together, the English are convinced that the full meaning of the word 'democracy' is unintelligible outside their frontiers, that the States of written law are inevitably subject to the reign of the arbitrary, and that justice is codified only the better to suppress it."*
**Philippe Daudy, *Les Anglais: Portrait of a People***

*"In the last analysis, the government's defense of the status quo boils down to little more than 'this is the way we've always done it.' As with so many things in Britain, that is precisely the problem."*
**Reginald Dale, *International Herald Tribune*, 4/6/1993**

*"The English are noted for their pragmatism, flexibility and short-term thinking. Frequently decisions are taken quite quickly without lengthy discussions, methodical planning, restrictive rules or 'red tape', based on the belief that one can proceed gradually ('incrementalism'), changing policies when necessary, or 'muddling through'."*
**Sir Christopher Leeds, Bt.**

*"My wife has two topics of conversation: the royal family and her bowels".*
**From the film *'A Private Function'*, quoted by Lynn Payer in her book *Medicine and Culture***

20

# Weak Uncertainty Avoidance

We English have reason to feel different from the people on the other side of the Channel. After all, many of the things that accompany us through our daily lives are different even if, more often than not, we are unaware of the fact. Of course, everyone knows that foreigners, with a handful of exceptions, drive on the right – though they may not know that it was that upstart Napoleon who had the original idea of changing sides because, in an era of right-handed coachmen, there was less chance of the whips getting intertwined.

Then there is the vexatious business of salt and pepperpots. We English – no, here I should associate all the British – put our salt in cellars with a single hole and our pepper in pots with lots of holes. Continentals, of course, do the opposite. I am not a specialist in saline mechanics, but it could be that a lot of little holes outperform a single large one when the hygroscopic salt gets sticky. But that's too logical.

English merry-go-rounds go clockwise, Continental ones anti-clockwise. The title on the spine of an English book standing on a shelf has to be read from the left, the title of a Continental book from the right. And so on...

In fact the differences go much deeper. You can explain the centuries-old mutual bafflement of the English and the French by simply remembering that we approach issues from opposite ends: we English tend to think inductively, from experience to principle, whereas the French think deductively, from principle to experience.

As American journalist Lynn Payer says in her fascinating book *Medicine and Culture*[5] Descartes, the father of cartesianism, aimed to evolve the universe from a thought, whereas "the British philosopher Francis Bacon urged society to try evolving thought from the universe." Indeed, both methods work well, in different circumstances.

The Englishman, it seems, likes theory in his medical thought no more than he does in his legal or political thought. No wonder the English and the French have difficulty in understanding one another.

Lynn Payer comes to the core of her research when she points out that the two cultures, like many others, differ fundamentally in their attitudes towards their bodies. We English are essentially bowel-oriented. We once fought a minor war (I haven't established when, where or against whom) to secure the supply of rhubarb. A couple of centuries ago, many of us drank a pint of seawater a day to ensure regular bowel movements.

In contrast the French, as everyone knows, are liver-oriented *(mon foie!)* and the Germans are cardiologically inclined *(Herzinsuffizienz, Kreislaufstörungen,* etc), even if they at times seem to be excessively bowel-oriented as well.

But to return to the thinking processes as opposed to the anatomical ones, in most cases – though I hasten to add not all – Continentals need to have a reason for doing what they do, where the English as often as not cite tradition and say 'because that's the way it is'.

"The whole of British law as well as government reflects this type of thinking", comments Payer in her book. "While on the Continent legal codes have been drawn up that anticipate disputes, in Britain law is based on the interpretations of cases that have already come up. While the vast majority of Western democracies have constitutions that outline *a priori* certain conditions of government, Britain has none, preferring to muddle along on principles derived out of experience."

Indeed, that's the way it is. And the tradition goes a long way back – though not much further back than anyone else's traditions. It also goes deep.

*'Don't worry, the au pair will clean it up'.*

A clever Dutchman, Geert Hofstede, worked out what was going on here. His findings[6], based on a mammoth research programme, showed that the different cultures – English, German, French, Dutch and so on – fall at different points on a series of common scales or 'dimensions'.

The most intriguing dimension is one he calls Uncertainty Avoidance. Here, the people of the British Isles come close to the bottom of the scale, only 'underperformed' by the Danes and Swedes (the German-speaking peoples come over half-way up, the Italians, Spanish, French and Belgians still higher, and the Portuguese and Greeks right at the top).

Hofstede concludes that the English, along with the rest of the British as it happens, feel comfortable with uncertainty.

We can live with it. The Strong Uncertainty Avoidance countries, on the other hand, have been brought up to avoid uncertainty. This need – which Hofstede and other sociologists attribute to the pervasive effect of Roman Law, which codified just about everything – has, over the centuries, become institutionalised. The presence of so many rules and regulations, in Latin countries in particular but also in Germany, has reinforced the individual's avoidance of uncertainty when he or she confronts it.

It is estimated that, strictly to stay within the law, an Italian should be aware of at least 800,000 regulations. Apart from being totally unmanageable as most things are in Italy, this means ironically that any self-respecting Italian finds ways of getting round the law. We English, from our standpoint, regard this as dishonest but, having accepted the Romans as unwanted guests for only a relatively short time by Continental standards, we have little reason to know what the Italians are putting up with.

What we do know is that the Continent – and what we perceive as 'Brussels' – can't kick this legislating habit and ultimately amounts to a very large row of brainless bean-counters and bureaucratic busybodies. To some extent we're right. But that doesn't mean to say that what we're doing is right too.

Where the German establishment keeps running to the constitutional court in Karlsruhe for a 'position' and even has a law called the *Notstandsgesetz* to fall back on when all other laws fail, the English establishment (plus a few Scots) make mealymouthed and meaningless appeals to freedom of speech and the like. Yet Britain still has to have a bill of rights (maybe it doesn't need one now, since its citizens have taken to appealing to the European Court). As Philippe Daudy says, "the use of *Habeas Corpus* as a means of defending individual liberties illustrates the deep-seated distrust of the English for ideas...".

In fact the English attachment to historical precedent, versus the Continental attachment to abstract principles, is probably the biggest difference between us and them. In most other respects, Continentals are actually not at all unlike us, except that they speak funny languages. They also have two eyes and two legs, operate in in-groups and even show a sense of humour of sorts. But, unlike the English, they generally don't like foreigners making jokes about them, although the Italians and even the Germans can tolerate a certain degree of leg-pulling.

We have something else in common. All of us, English and Continentals, are behaving like marionettes on 2000-year-old strings. Yet most of us are unaware of the way we are behaving, and even less of us know why. A prime example is Mrs T who was the voice of iconoclastic instincts, largely misread by the people-in-the-street, that seemed at the time to be serving the country well but ultimately led it into a dead-end.

It also seems to me that there is an urgent need to ask ourselves whether the 'British way of doing things' is so implacably and exclusively right. On the record since WWII, it seems not. Maybe there are some things Continentals do that we could learn from. Things like accepting a certain degree of codification of strategic areas of social activity, even the official monitoring of some sectors of the economy. The shibboleth of 'voluntary self-regulation' is losing much of its validity these days.

The fact that we are a Weak Uncertainty Avoidance people also shows up, of course, in the way we publicly assert our differences. Not only in the blatherings of Eurosceptics of all parties, but in the response of ordinary citizens to opinion polls. The Eurobarometer sounding mentioned in the previous chapter showed that, of the twelve countries in the European Union at that time, the British were the only ones confident enough to relate as a majority to their nationality (59%), while only 37% also felt themselves European. Even the Danes managed better (worse?) than this (50% – 50%), while the most European turned out to be the Italians (70%), the French and Belgians (65%), the Luxembourgers (63%) and the Dutch (59%).

Admittedly, feeling 'European' is an ill-defined thing, close to transcendental meditation... But, on the other hand, our ancestors came from Europe, the place that English people refer to when asking about the weather.

Or rather, as a friend pointed out, the sensible ones came across, the others stayed behind.

*"Derek Enright, a Labour MP, was signed up to make an album of Beatles classics in Latin. He was discovered after singing 'Yellow Submarine' in Latin in a Commons debate on education."* **The Economist, 29/5/1993**

*"The Parliament of Westminster has so successfully kept up the appearance of its past greatness, that it still believes in its reality. It has even managed to impart the belief to the rest of the world."*

**Philippe Daudy, *Les Anglais: Portrait of a People***

*"'What have you changed?', someone asked the prime minister, and Margaret Thatcher replied, 'I have changed everything.'"*

**Joel Krieger,
*Reagan, Thatcher, and the Politics of Decline***

*"The British are brave people. They can face anything, except reality."* **George Mikes, *How To Be Decadent***

*"Your concept of subsidiarity is fraudulent: you fail to have it on local and regional levels."*

**Jean-Pierre Cot, French socialist**

*"In Britain today it is very difficult to see other than mediocrity in public life."*

**William Pfaff, *Los Angeles Times*, 25/2/1993**

*"In order to reach for the truth the Germans add, the French subtract and the English change the subject."*

**Sir Peter Ustinov**

*"One of the British correspondents in Brussels says openly that the standing instruction from his editor is 'Send knocking copy'."*

**Sir Roy Denman, *International Herald Tribune*, 7/2/1994**

*"Humbug is alive and well in the British press."*

**Anthony Lewis, *The New York Times*, 5/7/1994**

# The show must go on

All Continentals – those people who live in a place often referred to as 'overseas' (come on, 22 miles away?) – talk about the eccentricity of the English. But many of them are not sure what they are talking about. We English are, after all, unworldly enough to defy explanation. We practice self-deprecation and spend an inordinate amount of time drinking tea, train-spotting and talking about the weather.

This, to us, is perfectly normal behaviour even if we do produce more eccentrics than anywhere else. According to Dr David Weeks of Scotland's Royal Edinburgh Hospital[7], the British – he's polite enough not to say the English – can claim twice as many fully blown eccentrics as the average for Continental countries, Slavs excepted of course.

But when Continentals talk about the eccentricity of the English they mean, quite simply, that we are different, which we take as a compliment. If they are under 40, they think we produce the best pop groups in the world. If they are over 40, their judgement is coloured by the conviction that despite all appearances to the contrary (pop groups, tourists, lager louts, Royal Family, etc) the true representative of the race is still the eccentric English gentleman – part Colonel Blimp or Pierre Daninos' Major Thompson, part bowler-hatted City Gent.

Continentals of that age-group may also be vaguely aware of his *alter ego* Andy Capp, the cloth-capped working man, not that there are many of him left. But what they all overlook is what used to be called the 'lower middle class', the C2s of the sociologists' world, the self-respecting rump of English society ('self-respecting' though, as George Mikes points out, absolutely no one gets any self-esteem out of calling him or herself 'lower middle class'...).

Although its outlines are hazier than they were – occupying a no-man's-land between what used to be called the working class and the rest – it is still a dominant if bland feature of British society, with its bungalows with funny names, its knicknacks and its startingly elliptic priorities and forms of speech.

If there is anything that justifies the claim that there are none as odd as the English, this is it. Whereas foreigners discurse logically and consequentially, the people inhabiting this stratum of what we wrongly call the English class system indulge in rabid non-sequiturs about things that would not be worth the time of day to anyone else.

There is something quite breathtaking and sublimely Pinteresque, about the mindless, even daft, inconsequentiality of their concerns and conversations. They even give their bungalows names like 'Dunroamin', 'Mon Abri' and 'Sai Wen'.

Upwardly mobile, the more fortunate ones now live in houses with names like 'Rippingtons', 'Magpies' and 'Whispers' (I have the list in front of me). Whatever persuaded the English that, in order to be fashionable,the name of anything they owned, home or shop, had to end with an 's'?

One can't pass over things like these without asking oneself whether they are not just a matter of English lower-middle-class folk psyche, but also a question of education? On the other hand a sociologist friend with whom I discussed this

*'Mark my words, there'll be all those foreign influences creeping in...'*

34

phenomenon believes that this ritualisation of speech and behaviour may result from the embedding or suppression of assumptions. "I think this is a source of great pleasure to the people who do it. The very act of assuming that you have an understanding with the person you are talking to – the person you are sharing assumptions with – is socially binding. English culture is strangely hermetic: you never have to explain yourself, except to a foreigner". Which, of course, it rarely occurs to the English to do...

Paradoxically the desire to appear different, a leitmotif of the English character, seems to be largely absent from this level of society. These good people want to be just like their peers, an insurance policy to help them through what all of them hope will be upwardly mobile lives.

But at other levels of English society, both above and below this transit zone, the desire to appear different is highly developed. Maybe it acts as an antidote to the stifling constraints of the so-called class system?

Mrs T's remark (see page 30) sounds like something straight out of 'Alice in Wonderland'. Maybe it is.

Clearly, though, the lady was taking herself very seriously at the time. Her words, which reflect an unnatural level of hubris, even by her standards, reveal another ambivalent quality of the English, a taste for showmanship (showwomanship in her case).

It can be claimed that showmanship is a natural extension of eccentricity. There's nothing wrong with showmanship *per se*, as long as the perpetrator knows it for what it is. In fact, a lot of Continentals would benefit by having more of this very human quality – and I am **not** thinking of the French when I say this.

The trouble is that English showmanship – the reverse side of our cultural 'coin', the obverse being understatement, which is inverted showmanship – can get the better of reality. Sometimes it descends to the level of flashy exhibitionism or even, simply, meretriciousness. It is depressing to discover how many public schemes turn out to be more style (verbal hype, modish symbols and other forms of window-dressing) than substance.

The urge to show off, to attract attention, never seems to be that far away. It contrasts with the tradition of cool reserve practised by many educated Continentals.

Even Mrs T's flair for playing to the gallery catalysed English triumphalism to create the optimism of the 1980s and the letdown that followed.

No doubt the relief of seeing ourselves released, if only temporarily, from the constraints of puritanism – a catharsis that hits English society every 50-100 years – is also a factor in the equation.

The need to show off may also be prompted by a sense of helplessness from our inability to cope with the world around us. I have seen periods when this frustration has expressed itself in a form of xenophobia, first in the 1970s and now today, when it may be a withdrawal symptom following the hubris of the Thatcher years.

Xenophobia is not an emotion that comes naturally to the English. Its most frequent and mildest expression is a begrudging, dog-in-the-manger attitude which does nobody any good. Yet it can get nasty, as when City yuppies show off their sense of exclusiveness and their bad taste by making fun of foreign visitors' accents.

Paul Theroux says of the English in his book *The Kingdom By The Sea*[8]: "They were not timid, but shy: shyness made them tolerant, but it also gave them a grudge against foreigners, whom they regarded as boomers and show-offs." Pot calling the kettle black!

Bad faith can also be a problem, particularly in the arena of public life: what the *Financial Times* calls the 'When-in-doubt-bash-a-Kraut' school of politics.

It seems that, in the exalted field of international affairs, we English have for a long time had a reputation for bad faith and, even more seriously, bad taste. This is a tradition our masters are anxious to maintain, and do so very successfully.

Part of the problem is the English fondness for rhetoric in public debate, where no holds are barred. As Peter Collett points out in his book *Foreign Bodies*[9], "the English do not like to appear opinionated – unless, of course, they are taking part in a political debate, where the normal rules of self-presentation do not apply, or in a TV chat show, where the medium demands strong opinions, even from people who don't have them."

THE BRITISH CHARACTER
FONDNESS FOR LAUGHING AT OUR OWN ANECDOTES

Rhetoric in debate and subtlety in negotiations are also encouraged by the sheer wealth of the English language. According to German linguists – and the Germans often get this kind of thing right – the English vocabulary contains somewhere between 600,000 and 800,000 words, technical terms excluded (they estimate German at 300-400,000 and poor little old French, rather surprisingly, at little more than 100,000).

It is obvious that most of us use little more than one per cent of the English vocabulary to communicate – the most frequently used words being 'nice' and 'lovely' – but, when getting one over those wily Continentals or simply trying to talk our way out of a corner, it's surprising how much more of this vocabulary comes into play. It's particularly surprising for foreigners.

As George Orwell pointed out in his 1946 essay *Politics and the English Language* [10], euphemisms, clichés and vague phraseology can be used to reinforce orthodoxy and defend the indefensible – something that the English establishment seems to be very good at doing.

Then there is the influence of Fleet Street. Foreigners are in awe at the power and authority of the British press. Printruns, which are enormous by Continental standards, cast an aura over the whole business, editorials included. The trouble is that the comment is often not what it would appear to be to an innocent foreigner, either because the popular press is scandal-mongering for scoops or is riding a politically inspired hobbyhorse.

Continentals don't expect this: with notable exceptions, particularly French, their press is sensible to the point of being mindblowingly dull. It wouldn't occur to them that what is being passed off as news is really comment. So, when the tabloids raged on about the irresponsibility of the unions and the laziness of the British worker in the 1960s and 1970s, the Continental media took them at their word and passed on the message that the Dear Old Country was going to the dogs. It was indeed, but it wouldn't have got there so fast but for the fact that the British media give it a hefty shove.

The media scene has witnessed massive changes since the 1960s, but the tradition of wilfulness, scoop mentality and irresponsibility is maintained, along with a growing inability to write clearly and spell correctly. This also applies to the readers of the tabloids: a pretty mindless audience has been handsomely supplemented by the subliterate hordes emerging from the educational system. A study done a couple of years ago found that half the readers of the stridently Tory Sun thought it was a Labour paper!

The lengths to which the popular press will go to sneer and smear is remarkable. Even the *Daily Telegraph* chose to characterise the perfectly well-intentioned COMA guidelines on healthy eating as "the food-Leninists' new onslaught".

Now the media are happily harassing the royals – only the boulevard press on the Continent often gets there first. More serious still, as Sir Roy Denman pointed out[11], English misconceptions about the Continent owe a lot to a press "a large part of which – the leading tabloid, and 60 per cent of the broadsheets – is owned by two nonresident foreigners who loathe Europe and ensure that their papers give it the same treatment as Pravda used to give the United States at the height of the Cold War."

It's curious to be saying these things about the media of a country which has no fundamental guarantees for freedom of speech!

*"No doubt the English fondness for animals, nature and rurality in a broad sense is due to the innate conservatism of many, and their preference for tranquillity, traditions, stability, continuity and the preservation of things associated with the past."* **Sir Christopher Leeds, Bt.**

*"I see no reason why the people of this country should have to change the habits of a lifetime, and of generations, just because we are members of the European Community."*
**Junior British Transport Minister defending the principle of driving on the left**

*"The monarchy remains the peak of a stultifying system of deference that still runs through British society. Americans defer to money, Frenchmen to brains, the British to social status... What sort of country do we want? Reproduction antique?"* **George Walden, MP**

*"When after months of travel, one returns to England, he can taste, smell and feel the difference in the atmosphere, physical and moral – the curious damp, blunt, good-humoured, happy-go-lucky, old-established, slow-seeming formlessness of everything."* **John Galsworthy**

*"The trouble is that very often the British love of what is ancient and well-known turns into fear of what is new and unknown."* **Beppe Severgnini, *The Economist*, 8/1/1994**

*"Newness – when it is not ridiculous – is somewhat gross."*
**Philippe Daudy, *Les Anglais: Portrait of a People***

*"There is certainly no equivalent of the Eurosceptic fury over the destruction wrought on a thousand years of constitutional perfection. Perhaps it is because these nations [the rest of the Twelve] enjoy no such tradition. No chaps in tights opening their parliaments."*
**James Morgan, *Financial Times*, 27/3/1994**

# The Nostalgia Factor

By rights, this should be the longest section of the book. In fact, it's the shortest. So much has been said about the English 'heritage hangover' that there's not much to add.

As an empirical people, eschewing theory in favour of experience, we English have an understandable fondness for tradition. We like what we know. The problem is that, in the process, we elevate tradition to the status of a religion.

Asked in a *Daily Telegraph* opinion poll[12] to say what they were proudest of about their country, 39% of respondents couldn't think of anything. The largest number of those who did have an answer said Britain's history or heritage.

'I'm backing Britain', to quote the slogan of an adoptive Great Britainer, or 'I'm looking back on Britain'?

Despite the inexorable modernisation of public life, hankerings after 'the way things used to be' are reflected in an unabated addiction to ceremony and symbolism. This has even been turned to good account with the lower orders, offering them an emotional alternative to the traditional bread-and-circuses or beer-and-skittles. All the prancing that goes on with wigs, knickerbockers and silly hats!

Often the ceremony seems hollow and meaningless, bereft of any contact with the life of today. But the manufacture of permanent unreality is, as journalist Nigel Fountain has described it, "a booming British industry".

Of course other nations have their ceremonial too (look at the French!), but the natives don't seem to be taken in by it in the same way. An example of ceremony at its best is the Brussels Ommegang: a careful historical reconstruction with the voluntary and enthusiastic involvement of all classes, nobility playing nobility and ordinary people playing the also-rans. Yet everyone knows it's a show and not the real thing.

Where the French establishment uses status and the trappings of authority as a lethal weapon in the battle for supremacy – often wielding naked power without the slightest attempt to dissemble – the English express it through a process of patronage, privilege and condescension. On the playing fields of British power, despite the evident symbolism, the use of status tends to be dissimulated – a typical bit of English fudge, again almost as if one were playing a game, just as MPs play games in the Lower House. The influence of the symbolic is sustained.

Closely linked to the taste for the symbolic is sentimentality – a pervasive and at times kitschy sense of nostalgia which grips so many Little Englanders (sentimentality and nostalgia grip a generation of Germans too, but that generation is dying out). English nostalgia is evident in the upsurge of cottage industries specialising in pot-pourri, petit point and variegated knicknacks, all packaged in floral patterns and pastel shades. Beatrix Potter's packaging was original and adorable, Laura Ashley's and Anita Roddick's looks derivative.

Nevertheless such things sell – and not just to Little Englanders. Foreigners love things like Minis, London taxicabs, double-decker buses, red telephone boxes, reproduction pub signs and, who knows, ghosts (in the words of author Andrew Green, "England is alleged to be the most haunted country in the world"). But we shouldn't let all this go to our heads: there are other things in life and death.

Moreover our heritage is not always what we believe it to be. Centuries-old tradition, be damned! England is a country where, in earlier days, women walked around with breasts exposed and teeth rotting in their heads; men meeting in the street, even strangers, kissed one another on the mouth; and, in refined society, it was considered bad taste to laugh.

Until the 18th century, England was an island of garlic-eaters and, until more recently, a place where the practice of queueing was unknown and the friendly neighbourhood milk-man unheard of. So much for nostalgia. Mythology would be a better word.

The same goes for our natural heritage. The English oak forests are a consequence of the uninhibited land clearance movements of the early Middle Ages. The Scots moors, treasured by travel connoisseurs for their distinctive landscapes, were once rich forest country. The tulip was only introduced to Europe from Turkey in the mid-16th century and our plane-trees arrived from the East in the 1700s.

So anyone who talks about 'our natural heritage', as if time had stood still all these centuries, is talking rubbish. As Paul Theroux says in his book, one of the few boasts the English risk is that their country is changeless. As if time stood still!

*"Electricity, fast trains, main drainage –*
*are you trying to ruin the amenities of the village?"*

*"In the bad old days it was common knowledge that the country was going to the dogs... what the right wing meant was that there were rail strikes every week; and what the left wing meant was that the country was run by a laid-back bunch of amateurs, who were never to be found during the 'season' because they were all at Ascot, Wimbledon or Glyndebourne.* Plus ça change.*"*

**William Keegan, *The Observer*, 25/6/1994**

*"The Jockey Club seems a microcosm of Britain's failings. Membership is by rank more than merit: its members include four princes, 25 peers, 18 knights, 14 military officers, five honourables, three sheikhs (admitted on sufferance since their horses were essential to keep racing going) and a judge."*　　　　　　**The Economist, 10/4/1993**

*"It is impossible for an Englishman to open his mouth, without making some other Englishman despise him."*

**George Bernard Shaw, *Pygmalion***

*"As long as you maintain that damned class-ridden society of yours, you will never get out of your mess."*

**Helmut Schmidt, German Chancellor**

*"The customary reward for a life spent in determined fight against privilege seems to be an elevation to the peerage."*

**George Mikes, *How to be a Brit***

*"Lady Lucinda has married various people, including a baronet called Sir Edmund John William Hugh Cameron-Ramsay-Fairfax-Lucy (son of Sir Brian Fulke Cameron-Fairfax-Lucy and of the Hon. Alice Buchan, daughter of Lord Tweedsmuir), thus becoming Lady Lucy Lucy. When she married Sir Peregrine Worsthorne (son of Colonel Koch de Gooreynd [who later assumed the name of Worsthorne], and of Lady Norman, and the brother of Simon Towneley [who assumed his surname in 1955 by royal licence and is now, of course, the Custos Rotulorum of Lancashire]) she became Lady Lucy Worsthorne.*

*"I cannot understand why foreigners find British nomenclature confusing."*　　**Dot Wordsworth, *The Spectator*, 14/5/1994**

# Of privilege
# and patronage

English nostalgia feeds on symbolism, and symbolism fuels English class consciousness, which has its ceremonial aspects as well. In fact symbolism is one of the mainstays of the class system, and often its only justification. It is the signals that decide things, not the substance.

In the words of the novelist David Lodge, "English social life is controlled by an intricate system of signals recognised by the natives." In fact, the so-called 'class system' is really a class signalling system designed to cope with the phenomenon of social osmosis and mobility.

What bemused Continentals and other foreigners have to understand is that the English class system is based on a lot more than income or even the bed you're born in. It extends to the way you speak (accent more than content), the way you eat your food and the way you dress. We English being what we are, we are polite enough not to comment openly on such things, but we register them meticulously.

Even if it has no justification, class consciousness is built into the English psyche. In the words of American author and journalist Flora Lewis[13], "acceptance, indeed assertion, of the right to class consciousness is too deep, almost as though class were an inalienable aspect of identity". It may be a uniquely English extension of the classification process that all mortals need, in order to cope with the seething humanity around them.

A British author, Andrew St George[14], has suggested that the English – specifically the Victorians who were English par excellence – invented the class system to make up for the lack of a written constitution! The resulting apparent hierarchy would generate the constraints lacking in an otherwise unstructured society. 'Social order' begetting social order, it seems.

But the so-called class system is by no means as finite as many of its victims imagine. **It is not even a system**. People know they are part of it without being sure where to situate themselves. If the current interpretation offered by a subsidiary of the MORI organisation and delicately entitled 'The Social Milieus in Great Britain' is anything to go by (see below), it's hardly surprising!

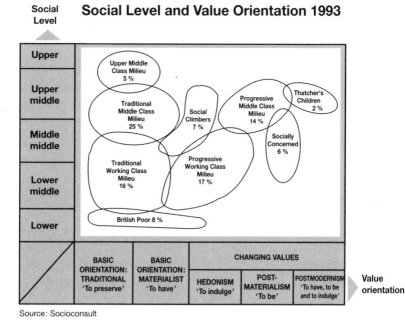

**Social Level and Value Orientation 1993**

Source: Socioconsult

On top of this, the damned thing has a habit of mutating subtly from generation to generation. I don't know how many sons of locomotive-drivers I have met who have become university graduates (Oxbridge included), successful entrepreneurs and rabid Tories. They keep the economy going. But their sons and daughters have an uncanny way of going back to their proletarian roots. The English class system is anything but rigid. It is highly permeable, both ways. But, at the end of the day, it is still there.

Another curious thing about it is that it helps reinforce attitudes at all points on the scale. Working class people – to be more exact, the people squashed between the mushrooming middle classes and the new underclass – are as proud of their identity as those better born or better off. Inverted snobbery always was a hallmark of the English.

George Mikes spotted this phenomenon back in the 1960s when he wrote *How to be a Brit* [15]: "Since the 'angry young man' literature made its impact, quite a few people assert that they are of lower origin than they, in fact, are."

In a MORI poll conducted in 1991 [16], while only 52% of the respondents said they identified themselves as working class (the official standard survey classification put the working class at 61% of the population at the time), no less than 66% of respondents said they preferred to be called 'working class'. Moreover this 66% represented a 50% increase on the national survey figures of 40 years earlier!

So this so-called class system is essentially a smoke-and-mirrors business. People slip out of one category into another like moulting chameleons. Take the case of Jeffrey Archer. Interviewed on French TV, he offered his elevation to the House of Lords as evidence of the absence of a class system! But it is precisely the willingness of clever individuals like him to be absorbed into the system that demonstrates its potency.

Paul Theroux saw another example of this on his journey around Britain: "There was a valley just west of where I was staying in which ardent socialists had settled and become landowners and country squires. They were union men or politicians who, after a career of howling at the rich, had been awarded knighthoods and appointed to directorships and had become well-to-do themselves. They lived in manor houses or on large farms, and some, amazingly, still espoused views that were in contradiction to the way they lived. It was a curious combination of secrecy, hypocrisy, and the sort of muddle that enabled an Englishman to hold two opposing views in his head."

*'Take him. He has a pad in the Dordogne, another in Tuscany and he's anti-EU'.*

The Queen's Birthday Honours List provides a perfect motivation and a well-oiled mechanism for social climbing. Those wise to the world know what it takes to get what. A presidency of one of the British Chambers of Commerce abroad is a free ticket to an OBE, even if you upset Her Majesty's Ambassador in the process by regaling a public luncheon with a series of blue jokes. *Noblesse oblige!*

Every European nation relies for its social and economic stability – and often its corruption – on a subtle structure of clubs or in-groups. Britain is no exception to this rule. The important thing is not what one knows but whom one knows. It is precisely because of this that, in a particularly class-conscious society like Britain, these in-groups mirror and at the same time reinforce class distinctions. In this sense they are particularly pernicious: rather than act as the motor for the revitalisation of the country, they act as a brake.

Consider the remarkably frank words, it seems devoid of irony, of the chairman of a well-known quango writing in his organisation's newsletter in 1991: "I became chairman [of the Countryside Commission] as a consequence of sharing a cab with a stranger. Another quango chairman was appointed following a pheasant shoot at which the secretary of state was a fellow gun; the subsequent chairman of a water authority bumped into a cabinet minister while birding on a Greek island [what kind of birds?]. It is a splendidly capricious and British way of doing things. I am advised that the success-failure rate is about the same as when headhunters are engaged. And look at the thousands of guineas you save". Guineas, eh?

The club mentality – and I am not just thinking of Boodles, far from it – comes very naturally to most self-respecting Englishmen. It has even prompted the Germans to call us 'the Sicilians of the North', an analogy that not only accommodates the fact that we both live on islands, but also the suspicion that we both have a Mafia.

Indeed the club (nay, the Mafia) mentality is well developed in Westminster's Lower House, aptly dubbed 'the temple of brown-nosing'. While more committed to professionalism, Whitehall is notorious as a gossip mill, another symptom of English clubbishness.

Gossip and the well-deserved English reputation for humour go well together (curiously, we have only one word, 'humour', to describe both wittiness and our state of mind, whereas the French have two, *humour* and *humeur*, though Theodore Zeldin[17] tells us that the *Académie Française* only admitted humour to the French vocabulary in 1932).

In fact, if you're English, you are well advised to show you have a sense of humour if you want to be taken seriously by your fellow-countryfolk. As Chris Powell says in his book *Humour In Society*[18]: "To get the joke and to respond appropriately demonstrates one's social competence, one's grip over and understanding of the way things are." Peter Collett concludes that "in England one can often get further in life with a sense of humour than with qualifications or talent."

Being part of the club, whichever one you choose, is intensely important to the English. Increasingly it manifests itself in the enthusiasm with which educated middle-class folk support special-interest groups lobbying for a better environment, a better deal for the poor or for the disabled, in short a better quality of life than government is offering.

Besides satisfying the 'club instinct' by helping them identify with people of the same kind, the phenomenon shows that there is still a strong reserve of compassion and concern in the English psyche.

These are meaningful manifestations of the club instinct. Others are a not-too-well-disguised act of self-preservation. But in most cases for the better-off, the resulting mood of gratification allied with patronage makes these things great fun.

It is nice to be amongst one's fellows and to share their prejudices. And the fact that these in-groups are motivated more by social considerations than serious ones only goes to prove what a sensible people the English are!

*"The change downward of England's intellectual life in the last 30 or 40 years has been pretty dramatic. We are much more parochial than we used to be and, so far as I can judge, much less well-read."*

**Norman Stone**, *The Guardian*, 13/6/1991

*"Income differences in the UK widened gradually until 1984 or 1985 when they suddenly started to widen very dramatically... There is evidence to suggest that health and educational performance are affected by relative deprivation through similar psycho-social channels."*

**Richard Wilkinson**, *Unfair Shares*

*"The British still cannot decide what they want education for. In Victorian times they were able to devise formidable new institutions like Imperial College to provide for a new technological world; but in today's world, which is changing much faster, they seem unable to connect education to the needs of the country, or any vision of the future."*

**Anthony Sampson**, *The Essential Anatomy of Britain*

*"The debate over teenage unemployment is, at bottom, a battle in the nascent civil war over what kind of society Britain should be, and what role the welfare state plays in it."*

**The Economist**, 4/6/1994

*"'Two nations: between whom there is no intercourse and no sympathy; who are as ignorant of each other's habits, thoughts and feelings, as if they were dwellers in different zones, or inhabitants of different planets; who are formed by a different breeding, are fed by a different food, are ordered by different manners, and are not governed by the same laws.'*
*'You speak of-' said Egremont, hesitatingly.*
*'THE RICH AND THE POOR'.*

**Benjamin Disraeli**, *Sybil*, 1845

# A people divided

The curse of class – on its own something that can be passed over with a gentle 'ah, well!' – is both directly and indirectly responsible for a rift in English society that goes much deeper. When examining the inability of the English to arrive at a social consensus, one is driven to the conclusion that the desire to be socially different is a major contributor to growing economic inequality.

The reason that German society has worked so superbly well since 1945, while English society has performed so peevishly, can be found in the words of Benjamin Franklin: "We must indeed all hang together, or most assuredly, we shall all hang separately". Far too many people in England are prepared to see their fellows go hang...

Or are they? The helplessness of people confronted with the present mess can lead to indifference. Yet indifference, as opposed to docility, is not an English characteristic. Sympathy for the underdog has always been a leitmotif of English life, even if it expresses itself in the upper classes as a rather condescending though well-meaning form of concern for those less well off.

But along came Mrs T. She saw the need to break out of the old system of patronage, but destroyed any spirit of consensus in the process. Not content with disrupting the old mechanisms that governed life in Britain, on both sides of the traditional class divide, she tore into the fabric of society. That fabric was already so weakened by in-fighting between the different factions that by the time she had finished, with the aid of some unfortunate initiatives and a lot of underfunding of such essentials as transportation and health care, there wasn't much left.

As historian Eric Hobsbawm said[19], "almost every bit of the moral consensus governing Britain for an awful long time has been outraged: the sense of fairness, the sense of *noblesse oblige* on the part of the upper classes, the sense that ordinary people can deserve something, and above all the sense that the community and the state have social responsibilities." It may have been paternalistic, but it was decent.

So we're back to Disraeli and Egremont, to the rich and the poor who, in some respects, reflect the country's geography, the North and the South. Sadly, however, the problem seems to be more institutionalised today than it was in Disraeli's time. The rich drive around in their smart cars with silly numberplates, while the poor – many of them young, unemployable and permanently marginalised – live in cardboard boxes. About 700,000 people were said to be homeless in 1990.

Even those supposedly more fortunate were suffering. By early-1994, the number of full-time British employees with weekly pay below the Council of Europe's 'decency threshold' had risen to 37%, compared with 28.3% in 1979[20]. New recruits to the country's growing underclass.

*"I said, we must have lunch some time ".*

between a poor North and a rich South is as marked as ever – even if a student of Indian descent said to me not long ago with great pride, "you know, we came through the recession a lot better than the South!", thereby demonstrating the power of the English culture to impose its values on others.

In his book *North and South* [21] David Smith comments that "even a recession as severe as that of the early 1990's cannot undo the effects of a century in which economic activity, and population, has shifted from North to South. What the recession undoubtedly did was to undo the sharp increase in North-South differences that occurred in the second half of the 1980s". This increase, which found its roots in the 1980-81 recession, had been fed by the expansionary and unstable economic policy of the Thatcher administration.

While the gap evoked by Disraeli is still there, it has changed in nature. A sociologist friend insists that, until the early-90s, the standard of living of most people had risen consistently since WWII. "What has happened in recent years is that the bottom 20% have fallen off the ladder. We therefore do not so much have an economic pyramid as an 'economic pear', with the stalk at the top. There are very, very few people who are extremely wealthy and a lot of people at the bottom who have gone backwards at an alarming rate and are still doing so. The government has taken to demonising sub-segments within this group, for example the work-shy and single mothers, and many government supporters, particularly those in the shires, find this demonisation a source of great comfort".

"It is this last point", he rightly adds, "that differentiates us so much from the Germans. They have an even more marked underclass but, while those who have emerged from it are indifferent, the mass of the German middle class reacts with deep concern. Britain does not come out of this comparison very well."

There is little evidence that the North/South gap will close – least of all in the inner cities of the smokestack belt – without a visionary act of long-term strategic investment allied with decentralisation. Unfortunately these are things that the Westminster/Whitehall establishment doesn't believe in.

Some recent studies suggest that there is a causal relationship not only between literacy and wealth, but also between wealth and health. The Northern Regional Health Authority[22] finds that death rates among men in the 45-54 age group in areas affected by poverty and unemployment are back to 1950s levels and are four times higher than in richer areas. The dramatic widening of income differentials since 1985 has not only partially **arrested** the decline in national death rates in all generations up to middle age, but has also brought with it a decline in the reading standards of schoolchildren.

The victims of these insidious trends can at least claim ownership of a new word in the English vocabulary: the 'underclass', defined in the shorter Oxford English Dictionary as "a class of people excluded by poverty and unemployment from any opportunity offered by society". Many of them risk being trapped in a vicious downward social spiral.

The words of Richard Wilkinson in the Barnardo's report *Unfair Shares*[23] are worth repeating here: "In the eyes of society how well-off you are appears as an expression of your ability and value as a member of society: implying that poorer people are of less account. This is closely related to the notion of respectability which, for many, is synonymous with social status and looking 'respectable'."

"Increases in relative poverty and deprivation affect the

sense of security among the majority of the population. The more unemployment, homelessness, houses repossessed and poverty there is, the greater will be the sense of anxiety and insecurity among the population at large... A less caring society redefines human relations... Where once the welfare apparatus of the state had stood as a clear statement of our mutual responsibilities to our fellow human beings, their decline now stands as a denial of that responsibility... The gradual transformation of a society, which had at least some of the attributes of a community which cared for its members, into a collection of individuals related only through the pursuit of material self-interest, leads to further decay of the social fabric."

The other symptom of this decay is illiteracy and low educational standards. According to *The Economist*[24], "in 1991, 62% of 16-year-olds in Germany, and 66% of them in France, gained the equivalent of a GCSE in three core subjects: maths, a science and the national language. The figure in England was a pitiful 27%. Nearly 15% of British 21-year-olds can barely read; 20% can't add up."

It is said that more than 6 million British people have problems with basic literacy and numeracy (one study puts the figure as high as 9 million). Seven out of ten job applicants at Nissan UK's factory, significantly located in Sunderland, fail to score 40% on the company's verbal reasoning test. [25]

The *Sunday Times* delved into this top layer of the educational deficit in March 1993 with the comment that "the erosion of literacy is a national issue." In support of this claim, the paper offered the following as proof: more than half

Britain's office workers can't spell the word 'innovate'; nearly half can't choose between 'brake' and 'break'; many of today's graduates score below the average 1977 16-year-old in grammar; and one in three sixth-formers misspells 'foreign' and 'initials'.

In February 1994, the Adult Literacy and Basic Skills Unit (ALBSU) published the results of a study conducted among 1,650 young English and Welsh adults aged 21. [26] This showed that 43% of the sample failed on some communication tasks (English speaking or writing) and 54% failed on some numeracy tasks considered essential in one in four 'lower and middle level jobs'. The implication was that they were virtually unemployable. The authors remarked that many of those with low literacy skills "are effectively marginalised in education and then confined to unskilled jobs, training schemes and lengthy periods of unemployment."

The study, which noted the preponderance of children from educationally disfavoured parents in this category, concluded that "the research shows the serious problems with essential basic skills a significant minority of young people have in England and Wales. A substantially larger number of young people seem to perform at a lower level than is required by the demands of everyday life and work in a developed, industrialised country like the UK."

Falling standards of literacy are not just an English concern: the problem exercises the authorities in other parts of Europe. But when one realises how much more articulate the young in Germany or France – or Scotland, for that matter – are when talking about serious things like current affairs or politics, one senses that the issue goes far deeper than the mechanistic aspects of communication.

Government educational policy since 1945 has been an unbroken sequence of muddle and change, albeit rightly prompted by the desire to break down class attitudes without creating a meritocracy. The latest modifications to the National Curriculum are an improvement, with the emphasis back on basic skills, but the idea of more teaching of English history sounds like true Little Englandism. And we are going to have at least one lost generation on our collective conscience.

On second thoughts, more than one: Welsh mothers are now having to resort to buying their toddlers second-hand shoes. They can't afford new ones.

*"The English are by nature a compromising and even a vacillating people."* **H G Wells, *The Outline of History***

*"The British character is too much against revolution, or even logical consistency, drastic steps, and uncompromising action."*
**Nikolaus Pevsner, *An Outline of European Architecture***

*"The British are notable for their sentimentality, which they mistake for a virtue: hence their ability to deceive themselves, which others mistake for hypocrisy."*
**Lord Hailsham**

*"Speaking to strangers was regarded as challenging in England; it meant entering a minefield of verbal and social distinctions."* **Paul Theroux, *The Kingdom By The Sea***

*"The English people on the whole are surely the nicest people in the world, and everyone makes everything so easy for everybody else, that there is almost nothing to resist at all."* **D H Lawrence, *Dull London***

*"One of the reasons why the English are so reserved is that they have a deep-seated desire not to impose themselves on other people, and not to be imposed upon by others."*
**Peter Collett, *Foreign Bodies***

*"Bargaining is a repulsive habit; compromise is one of the highest human virtues – the difference between the two being that the first is practised on the Continent, the latter in Great Britain".* **George Mikes, *How To Be An Alien***

*"For all their simulated modesty, the British can be tough and blandly ruthless when necessary. They are masters at intelligence gathering, political blackmail, and chicanery..."*
**Philip Harris and Robert Moran,
*Managing Cultural Differences***

# Consensus
# and confrontation

The English are complex and perplexing. They are complex as individuals and complex as a group. Every European culture draws on people of widely varying personalities, but the English culture is also fragmented by social distinctions. Where the Germans as a community find reassurance in their similarities, the English, with the marked exception of the middle class, seek refuge in their differences.

Philippe Daudy speaks in his book about the "individualism and docility which I believe to be the basic characteristics of English society". These 'basic characteristics' are contradictory. Individuals are supposed to stand up for their rights. Yet, more often than not with the English, social docility gets the upper hand. While they are anything but indifferent, people don't challenge authority, even when it grossly abuses the principle of fairness.

Speaking of fairness, there's another English idiosyncrasy. Indeed Continentals, who regard the principle of fairness as admirable but slightly daft, have had to import the word 'fair' since there is nothing that matches it in their own vocabularies (they have also imported the word 'partner', which the Germans use excessively in advertising slogans).

Quite simply, the English are not of revolutionary stock. A friend of mine says that English society is skilled in absorbing dissidents: he thinks the only grassroots rebellion of the last 50 years was the Campaign for Real Ale. Indeed I have had many Continentals say that, with the way the country has been mismanaged since WWII by almost all concerned, it's a miracle we haven't had a revolution. But we haven't.

These English qualities – individualism and docility – have their downside. Individualism, when given full rein, can lead to overweening self-interest or flashiness. Docility, when abused by others, turns quickly into resentment.

Docility is also a reflection of inherent shyness. As Paul Theroux says, once again in the past tense: "The English were tolerant in the sense that they were willing to turn a blind eye to almost anything that might embarrass them. They were humane, but they were also shy."

According to Peter Collett, who is a research psychologist at Oxford University, this shyness is largely motivated by the desire not to be disliked, in contrast to the Latin's desire to be liked: "Because the English place disproportionate emphasis on negative, rather than positive evaluation, they are much more likely to experience shyness than, say, the Italians, who place relatively greater emphasis on positive rather than negative evaluation."

The English can be both conciliatory and ambitious. They can be fair and full of humbug, decent yet deceitful. It is surprising how many 'bromide' verbal formulas are used to cope with the discomfort of expressing an adversarial opinion. Phrases like 'if I may say so', 'with great respect', or the opening remark of a traffic policeman to a speeding motorist: "I'm afraid, sir, you have committed an offence". In the words of Margaret Atwood, a Canadian novelist, "I know the British are famed for their plots, not saying what they really mean".

Often it's just to spare the other person's feelings – and there's nothing wrong with that. But if the English psyche finds a frustration or a provocation too hard to bear, it can overreact violently, often to the owner's surprise.

Like all European cultures the English version conceals inner contradictions or 'psycho-poles'. A change in mood or context can trigger a sudden shift from one pole to the other. Robert Louis Stevenson, a Scotsman, made a nod to his neighbours when he conjured up Dr Jekyll and Mr Hyde.

Misled by our generally relaxed behaviour as a Weak Uncertainty Avoidance culture, Continentals often interpret the English desire to avoid confrontation not as politeness, which it often is, but as hypocrisy.

George Mikes said, "if you want to be really and truly British [I would have said English], you must become a hypocrite". The impression can easily be encouraged by such small and relatively innocent things as the businessman's bromides of 'we must have lunch sometime' or 'I'm thinking about it'. But it is occasionally reinforced by what can only be interpreted as acts of pure duplicity.

*'We've been waiting to see how the European Union summits go before we decide'.*

Our neighbours have difficulties in equating the English sense of compromise with the televised goings-on in the Lower House. When our elected representatives behave in such an aggressive and ill-mannered way in public life, it is difficult for Continentals to believe that the English are as reasonable as they pretend to be. In fact some of the best demonstrations of naked ambition in play are to be found in the constant jockeying for position in parliamentary life.

The adversarial nature of the political scene, and to some extent the conduct of British justice, stand out in stark contrast to our normal predilection for compromise. Yet one is a consequence of the other. But the political tradition has tragically led us to believe that consensus as a social doctrine is for the birds – or for Continentals.

In the words of *The Economist*[27], "the British, used to the idea that politics is about confrontation, have come to view consensus as somehow suspect." Indeed we seem to be blind to the evidence coming from across the Channel that the will to foster consensus between the different components of society can produce beneficial results.

In international politics the English sense they are 'on stage' and behave accordingly. As Ruud Lubbers, Dutch prime minister at the time, said of English so-called negotiating tactics: "I am worried that there is a tradition that it feels good to say 'No'". The most recent example was the vetoing of Jean-Luc Dehaene's candidacy as President of the European Union, which was not only tasteless but destructive.

Despite such demonstrations of bad taste and bad faith, the English are generally well-meaning: this is only a mild criticism. But sometimes they are not: this is a much more serious criticism because, when they are not, they are absolutely perfidious. Incidentally it was a Spaniard, not a Frenchman, who used that word about Albion.

In his book *The Europeans*[28], Italian journalist and author Luigi Barzini talks about the ability of British statesmen to "resort with equal ease and elegance to what seemed to foreigners Levantine duplicity, Greek ambiguities, Florentine intrigues and, but more rarely, outright treachery. This unexpected flexibility", he adds, "offended the French in particular, perhaps because they alone felt entitled to resort to such dubious techniques."

Ask the Americans how they feel about British tactics on the occasion of and after the GATT audiovisual deal. Evidently things haven't changed. Only, in this case, the so-called 'special relationship' is at stake...

*"What Britain did, under the historical aberration known as 'Thatcherism', was to overreact, and to fashion, as a deliberate aim of policy, a country where anarchy and lack of accountability were the norm..."*

**William Keegan, *The Observer*, 26/6/1994**

*"It is beginning to be hinted that we are a nation of amateurs."*

**Earl of Rosebery, British Prime Minister, 1900**

*"Since deregulation, large financial conglomerates have been formed. They operate within a loose legislative framework, optimistically relying on self-regulation by the institutions' own trade associations and professional bodies."*

**John Mole, *Mind Your Manners*, 1990**

*"The English temperament feels uncomfortable in a world where predictability, mechanical determinism and machines seem to be taking over and conditioning men's lives."*

**Sir Christopher Leeds, Bt.**

*"The question one asks again and again about the British is, why will they not take themselves seriously?"*

**William Pfaff, *Los Angeles Times*, March 1993**

*"There is a tendency to believe information is a dangerous commodity, that it is somehow subversive".*

**Shaun Leslie, Association for Geographic Information**

*"When things go seriously wrong in England, you can be sure of two things. First of all someone will make a cup of tea, and then the same person, or someone else, will crack a joke."*

**Peter Collett, *Foreign Bodies***

*"Like many of his compatriots, he [Mr Major] regards 'vision' as a dirty word. He is the ultimate short-term thinker."*

**Reginald Dale, *International Herald Tribune*, 1/3/1994**

*"The English instinctively admire any man who has no talent and is modest about it."*

**Attributed to James Agate**

74

# The importance of being unaccountable

**W**illiam Keegan (see page 74) hit the nail on the head – even if 'accountability' was a parrot-cry of Thatcherite politicians.

While the principle of accountability was cheerfully forced down the throats of schoolteachers, scientists and hospital administrators, it was strikingly absent from government and some privileged sectors of society.

As Anthony Sampson says in *The Essential Anatomy of Britain*[29], "the gap between government and governed looms wider than ever, and Britain is run by one of the most centralised and least accountable systems in the industrial world."

Untrammelled by the regulatory influences of the Roman Empire, still so alive in many Continental countries, and emboldened by our Weak Uncertainty Avoidance, we English are allergic to anything that strikes us as being over-organised.

The result is that we have a mild disdain for professionalism in any form. This is linked with a distaste of anything smelling of ambition or success. Indeed, as a friend points out, in English society the penalties for failure are much more important than the rewards of success. Not that David Frost, described by Richard Ingram as "a young man so obviously on the make", has failed to see his ambitions rewarded by being tolerated by the establishment and sucked up (an appropriate phrase!) into the class system.

The worst offence of all, as George Mikes has pointed out, is 'cleverness'. He learned this when an English lady commented "you foreigners are so clever." At first, he thought it was a compliment, but he quickly changed his mind. Smart guys are still out of fashion today, at least in the upper echelons of the social order.

Peter Collett pursues this point: "When the English are judging other people they tend to place more emphasis on character than on brains. In fact intellectual prowess is frequently regarded as a disadvantage, something to be hidden rather than put on display where it might show up other people. After all, it was the English who produced expressions like 'too clever by half' and 'too clever for his own good', which carry the clear message that intelligence isn't necessarily a good thing."

I wouldn't go so far as to say that we are an island of self-proclaimed amateurs, though this used to be the case somewhere between the Victorian era and today. We are beginning to understand that pinning the flag of amateurism to our mast is perhaps not such a clever thing after all – even if we still disdain those who take their professionalism too seriously.

There is, happily, growing evidence that the cult of the amateur is on the way out, and thank god for that. It had a very seductive, and generally destructive, influence on English life. Amateurism nearly destroyed UK industry, well before the 'winter of discontent'.

Some sectors of society, however, are relatively resistant to the virus of amateurism, the Scots for a start. With some notable exceptions, professionalism has always been the hallmark of the senior ranks of the Civil Service, unlike their political masters. It is also endemic in the financial and service sectors of the economy. Fortunately it is now extending into manufacturing, what is left of it.

Quite rightly, we English have a visceral hate of bureaucracy – the 'B-word' that alliterates with, but is not confined to, Brussels – and of intervention or institutionalisation in any form (although, in parenthesis, Britain has one of the best records on the ratification and implementation of EU directives). All of this is only to be expected of people with Weak Uncertainty Avoidance.

But, in our loosely structured minds, many of us allow these hatreds to spill over onto anyone or anything betraying a sense of vision. Even self-interested long-termism, implying a moral (or immoral) commitment and the necessary controls and administration to render the project effective, makes us feel uncomfortable. As a German negotiator said at the time of the Single European Act, pre-Maastricht: "we knew it was another step towards an ever closer union, but the British never look ahead". Look at what has happened since!

It is astonishing that this country, inherently and congenitally resistant to doctrinaire thinking, should have been so bemused by a prime minister who is the most doctrinaire personality to have moved centre-stage in many years. And, as *The Economist* pointed out [30], "why was a politician who celebrated the individual over the state such a relentless centraliser of government power, and so careless of civil liberties?"

In the process of denigrating any *Weltanschauung* other than our own, we dispose of the smart guys, the intellectuals and the institutionalisers and we deify the amateurs, the pragmatists and the self-regulators. Amateurism is the enemy of accountability.

Naturally, for a Weak Uncertainty Avoidance people, we detest what we perceive as unnecessary legislation and opt for self-regulation wherever we can – regardless of the mounting evidence that self-regulation only works where the self-regulators act in a professional and responsible way.

This shibboleth of self-regulation is a good example of the doctrinairism, untypical for the empirical English, that is now holding the country hostage. A recent example is the reluctance of the government to regulate the private security service industry, despite the pleas of both the police and the industry itself. It is difficult to see how a business sector that accommodates new entrepreneurs straight from prison can be expected to self-regulate!

Anthony Sampson talks about the irresponsibility, the evasiveness and "the shams behind much of the City's self-regulation... It was the ability of individuals to pass the buck which lay behind all the City scandals, whether in the banks, the boardrooms or the Bank of England." To which one can add the Lloyds debacle, where an explosive mixture of incompetence, complacency, wishful thinking and greed blew up in everyone's faces.

Denis Brulet, the French managing editor of AFP-Extel News, offers us a Continental's interpretation of English

*"What do you mean, Them? We are Them."*

business ethics: "The notion that business law is not an exact science is also something useful to bear in mind when doing business in London. Indeed, the highly ambiguous formulae invented by City businessmen through the centuries seem to have one main purpose: to save them from finding themselves with their backs against the wall. If these fail, a City businessman will resort to the most flagrant dishonesty and specious arguments to avoid the above humiliation." So much for self-regulation.

The recent record of the judiciary in enforcing regulations where they exist hasn't been too brilliant either. Undermined by some notorious cases of miscarriage of justice that have come to light in recent years, public confidence in the judiciary has never been lower in a country which used to show intrinsic respect for the law.

A poll conducted with a sample of 970 UK citizens in 1993[31] showed that 61% of those questioned, regardless of age and class, no longer believed it was possible to get a fair trial in Britain today. Not altogether surprising when, in the words of *The Economist*, "the way judges are chosen is Kafkaesque". Byzantine might be a more appropriate word.

A foreign observer, Philippe Daudy, concludes that "no democratic country, apart from England, would dare to select such an important category of people under so arbitrary a procedure." No wonder that more and more ordinary people are appealing to the European Court of Justice for redress!

As Mrs T said in an interview with the *Financial Times*, "like most people in this country I am suspicious of blueprints, especially where institutions are concerned". It seems that we English cannot bear institutionalisation in any form.

We want to be ourselves, with freedom of speech, freedom of thought, freedom to screw things up and, it seems, freedom to go to rot.

*"This [the automobile industry] is merely an example of a general tendency Britain is suffering from – multiple self-inflicted wounds... Britain's workforce is intrinsically second to none but it has been humiliated for what it was and mistreated for what it has become."*

**Peter Ustinov, *The European*, 22/10/1992**

*"The quite explicit ultimate aim of a European federation was the best kept secret in Whitehall since D-Day.*
*The British joined the Community to sell marmalade and cotton underwear."*

**Sir Roy Denman, *International Herald Tribune*, 22/7/1993**

*"Up to 80 per cent of the appointments to the boards of large British companies are still made on the old boy network."* **1992 corporate governance report quoted by Anthony Sampson**

*"Qualities sought for in future managers used to be based on those associated with the so-called gifted amateur or gentleman all-rounder. He would be expected to be an improviser, quick-witted or intelligent rather than intellectual. He would learn his job 'by doing' or from experience rather than through formalised special training or higher education."* **Sir Christopher Leeds, Bt.**

*"The British seem to have convinced themselves that selling key industries to the highest bidder shows that the nation is in tune with the modern world of international capital, and with British membership in the European Union. They seem out of touch with the real world of industry and commerce – a world beyond the financial engineering and corporate trading that dominate British business, with its City of London orientation."*

**Philip Bowring, *International Herald Tribune*, 23/2/1994**

*"What British industry needs to do is to challenge every principle it has used in the past."*

**Perry Offer, Managing Director,**
**Hartstone Hosiery Manufacturing**

82

# Is Britain working?

W hen I arrived in Belgium in 1967 to start an international service business, I brought a book with me called *What's Wrong With British Industry?* by Rex Malik[32]. A sense of national crisis was already in the air. Many books have been written on the same subject since, most of them saying much the same thing.

I also brought with me the fond idea that, with blood thicker than water, I should look to my compatriots to give my fledgling business a fair start. No such luck. Apart from the fact that my employers gave me an almost derisory subsidy of £4,000 for the first year of operation (admittedly the £ bought 120 Belgian francs in those days) and then persecuted me with operating standards which were totally irrelevant to conditions here (something many British companies still delight in doing), I had overestimated the fellow-feeling of my fellow-countrymen.

I had also overestimated the British presence in what is a small but friendly and open market, one regarded by many international companies as the ideal test market for pan-European operations. It wasn't long before I realised that, outside consumer goods, financial services and real estate, there was no coherent British presence, least of all in industrial or high-technology products, with the exception of one or two multinationals. The country was simply losing out by default.

The country has since been losing out to the extent that, in the last 20 years, while Britain's manufacturing output has stagnated, Germany's has grown by 25%, France's by 27% and Italy's by 85%. During the Thatcher era, between 1979 and 1988, the ratio of imports to total manufacturing output increased by over 31.2%, reflecting a rise in manufactured imports of no less than 98.7%.

The sad record of British industry both at home and 'overseas' is explained in part by class attitudes. You simply didn't send your son (or daughter) into industry. But class, English-style, is also closely linked to another phenomenon which has bedevilled British business for far too long, the cult of the amateur – something that has also been called "the contempt of the squirearchy for useful knowledge."

Closely related as it is to the British taste for eccentricity, this cult has blossomed since Victorian times. It is strange how Britain revered its engineers in the 19th century (the most famous of whom, Brunel, happened to be a Frenchman), only to treat them with little better than contempt in the 20th.

Talking to *International Management* magazine Akio Morita, chairman of Sony, expressed his surprise that some British manufacturing companies are led by chief executives "who do not understand the engineering that goes into their own products. This strikes me as very curious...".[33]

*"How do you like being on the board of directors, Wilkinson?"*

This dilettante attitude reflects the inborn snobbery of some sections of society as well as a predilection, among those that can afford it, for a liberal education with the emphasis on 'learning the business of life' rather than a vocational one. As *The Economist* says [34], "Britain's education system undervalues practical skills. This has hit manufacturing hard. The brightest are taught superbly well at university. But those who do not go to university enter the job market with few useful qualifications."

English society has also encouraged a form of class discrimination, conscious or unconscious, to the detriment not only of engineers, but of technicians generally and (as in the case of the French) salespeople. Today, Britain even spurns science as a vocation.

A Spanish academic, José Luis Alvarez, comments that "despite the successes of the industrial revolution, in Britain aristocratic values remained dominant, including some disregard and contempt for business activities."

Klaus Schmidt, a German researcher, finds that "some Britons view the process of buying and selling – the very concept embodied in world trade – with misgivings. The visitor who has to come to Britain to sell must overcome this attitude." That is very much the attitude of the old school, but it does still persist at some levels of British society.

In the article referred to above, *The Economist* explains this state of affairs in the following terms: "The British appear to scorn manufacturing. Graduates prefer to become lawyers, financiers or journalists [rather surprisingly, a survey undertaken by the Egon Zehnder consultancy found that the percentage of law graduates was even slightly higher in British than in German top management]. Other studies show that students in Germany are almost four times as likely as British students to consider a career in manufacturing. This cultural bias in Britain against such 'grimy' jobs may just reflect

Britain's longstanding comparative advantage in trade, finance and other services (hence higher pay in those areas), or it may be a cause of it."

The rather casual sale of Rover to BMW – dismissive of both the British public and the Japanese management of Honda – was indicative of this mindset. An opinion piece in the *International Herald Tribune*[35] remarked that "the Rover episode is a telling comment on Britain's disinterest in manufacturing, its complacent belief that it can make a living from services and low-wage industries owned by others."

In stark contrast to Continental attitudes, English attachment to the cult of the amateur encourages a mistrust of anyone suspected of precociousness or, funnily enough in the circumstances, overt ambition. The country in fact offers more opportunity to the self-taught than a thoroughly elitist society like France, but there is still a degree of scorn in certain circles towards the 'self-made' man or woman.

An early-1994 study by Coopers & Lybrand of the so-called British 'Middle Market' – companies with turnovers from £8-500 million – concluded that, while owner-managers enjoy a position of respect in Germany, their British counterparts, especially those in manufacturing, do not get the recognition they deserve. Two-thirds of respondents felt that government policies and the 'roller coaster' economy were a hindrance to business success, and four-fifths blamed short-termism by the City as the biggest single factor contributing to British industry's decline.[36]

Despite its rather vicious value system characterised by greed, the City's Yuppie generation has indeed shown the country that we English can take business seriously. When we do so, we summon up reserves of creativity and resourcefulness that should turn any Continental entrepreneur green with envy or yellow with funk – as seems to be the case at the moment with the German insurance companies.

# The Road to Oblivion

*The lost marques
of the British motor industry*

1955  Lancaster (liquidated)

1959  Standard (liquidated)

1969  Riley (liquidated)

1970  Vanden Plas (liquidated)

1971  Austin-Healey (liquidated)

1975  Wolseley (liquidated)

1984  Morris (liquidated)

Triumph (liquidated)

1987  Austin (liquidated)

1989  Jaguar/Daimler (sold)

1992  Bedford (sold)

1993  Leyland (management buyout)

1994  Rover/Landrover/MG (sold)

Most of the UK motorcycle industry
went down the same road.

The potential for corporate entrepreneurship is evident in the performance of companies like BA, British Steel and particularly consumer goods giants like Allied Lyons, Cadbury Schweppes, Grand Metropolitan and Unilever. English creativity is also very much in evidence in the service and entertainment sectors: financial services, retailing (notably Marks & Spencer), advertising, TV and pop music.

But the country has seen many big names surrender to better organised, more energetic competition. In the engineering sector, significantly, whole industries have been decimated or wiped out entirely in recent years: car manufacture, although we still have fine components companies and absolutely dominate the rest of the world in high-tech automotive engineering; machine-tool manufacture; and most recently the forklift truck industry which, despite world-class design and production skills, succumbed to lack of scale and undercapitalisation.

Despite its own successes, the City is a villain in the drama of British decline. Speaking of British 'short-termism' Gottfried Bruder, general manager of the London branch of Commerzbank, says that "the entire financial culture in the UK and its effects on industry are such that, taken together, they constitute a strong disincentive for investment in any form that cannot almost instantly provide returns pleasing to the stock-market." There speaks a German!

Clive Dolan, the head of an electronic systems company acquired by the German Siemens group from Britain's Plessey, makes the same point [37]: "What Plessey did most of the time was respond to the City of London's need for quarterly profit increases. The British electronics industry hasn't done well globally because they've had their eyes on the wrong ball. Sensible long-term plans were disrupted constantly by short-term considerations."

The result is that, today, there is no UK-owned organisation that can claim a leadership position in any area of computer technology, hardware, componentry or software. Britain has only ten software companies that can be regarded as successful, and most of these have achieved this by moving to the USA!

The country's age-old reputation for under-investing is ironically borne out by the experiences of a growing number of industries that have been acquired by foreign organisations like Siemens: investment ratios have doubled and, suddenly, they have become successful in the marketplace. If their equations had been right, while they were still independent, they would never have been bought out!

In the 1980s, Britain was the only one of the fourteen member-countries of the OECD to register a fall in investment in non-defence research as a percentage of GNP. Yet ironically, as David Coates points out in his book *The Question of UK Decline*[38], since WWII the country has invested a larger share of R&D expenditure on military projects than any of the other major industrial nations.

The hallmark of the English mind is pragmatism or, more explicitly, empiricism. In the flux of today's business environment, this characteristic can be helpful in coping with change – even if it does at times metamorphose into a swashbuckling and sometimes flashy style which alarms more sedate senior managers in Continental industry.

Being free of the psychological constraints associated with the highly codified societies of many Continental countries, the 'Weak Uncertainty Avoidance' English are well equipped to accommodate change – the constant we now have to live with. According to a study undertaken by French researcher Jacques Horovitz[39], top British managers give more time to strategic problems than to daily operations: the opposite applies in Germany and France.

This is in stark contrast to the attitudes of the political establishment which reveres pragmatism to the point that 'vision' ranks as a dirty word – along with, to the English, emotive labels like 'bureaucracy', 'federalism' and the like. Regrettably, the nearest it has come to vision of any kind in recent times is Mrs T's return to Victorian values and the concept that, as Francis Kinsman puts it in his book *Millenium*[40], "individual power is good and collective power is corrupting".

Whether we English can exploit the unique opportunity that circumstances now offer us remains to be seen. I have a lingering suspicion that, with our dedication to short-termism, we will let the opportunity pass us by.

Yet there could be hope of our recovering the entrepreneurial spirit of the Victorians, as evidenced in the uprush of grassroots SMEs (small and medium enterprises) in the last few years. Sadly many of these then got knocked on the head by cashflow problems and high interest rates. Bankruptcies peaked at 63,000 in 1992.

The relatively freewheeling behaviour of the average English executive, when compared with his or her Continental equivalent, lends itself naturally to such challenging situations. The American in charge of the European subsidiary of a US software company comments that "the British are very creative software designers, but there are always some bugs – we leave it to the tunnel-vision guys to fix it."

This creativity is also evident in the revitalising impact that the more professional British managers could have, and actually have had, on the life of multinational corporations. Baldwin Klep, a partner with the Heidrick & Struggles executive search consultancy, believes that the British contribution to the present cadre of multinational managers is as important as that of any other country.

The new generation of English managers certainly get top marks from their Continental peers for their teamwork and also their ability to motivate and lead people. These qualities are evident in the dominance by the English of one of the fastest-moving industries in the world, Formula One.

This is, of course, precisely the environment that encourages the ambitious. The CEO referred to above comments rather cruelly: "The trouble is that, now that they no longer have an empire, they all want to build empires of their own." Worse than that, many of the old school are simply poorly motivated or incompetent. A British computer consultant says, flatly, "80 per cent of UK managers are not even worth talking to."

Hardly surprising when, as David Coates says in his book, "the broad recruitment pattern of UK management this century has been programmed to reproduce industrial conservatism and status anxiety in the middle ranks of the managerial hierarchy: denying middle managers the protection of formal qualifications and professional standing, yet subordinating them to senior strata who are visibly the scions of wider patterns of privilege and status". That corrosive mix of class and amateurism!

One thing is clear however: there is a world of difference between the traditional British businessman and the younger executives, men and women, rising through the ranks today. The English do indeed work these days. Executives are earning a reputation as 'the workaholics of Europe' – a genuinely respectful acknowledgement proferred by Continentals – even if the change in attitudes reflects the effects of downsizing and the need to catch up with the rest. There is ample evidence that we are working much harder and with more determination than we used to. Times have changed!

A British consultant, who has lived outside the country for more than 20 years but works regularly for British high-technology corporations, has witnessed the change from an objective standpoint: "The middle management in British hi-tech industries used to be awful: they were poorly educated and poorly motivated. Today people working up the ladder, those in their 40s and early-50s, are far superior in education, ability and performance. They are also harder-working than many Continentals and they certainly work longer hours."

"But", he adds, "British top management is still too elitist... and often amateurish." That word again!

*"The beach was undeniably lovely and unspoiled, but at this western end of it were peeling, collapsing huts and rusting caravans and weeds and even a dump full of twisted metal and yesterday's plastic – this disfigurement was reminiscent of a third world country, where they did not know any better, and just let the detritrus pile up as evidence that this rubbish was another aspect of civilization. It struck me that as time passed some countries with nothing in common but poverty would begin to resemble one another, because, while great civilizations are often vastly different and each culture is unique, everyone's junk is just the same."* **Paul Theroux, *The Kingdom by the Sea***

*"In some respects, Britain in recent years has given the foreign visitor the impression of an East European or Third World country. Its transportation systems are deplorable and neglected, the streets dirty, contemporary buildings and shops dreary and ugly. This is less the result of the country's economic problems – Britain, after all, remains very rich by East European or Third World standards – than of recent governments' ideological hostility to public spending."* **William Pfaff, *Los Angeles Times*, 25/2/1993**

*"If there were a prize for the worst-run major Western economy over the past 30 years, the long-suffering citizens of the United Kingdom would probably unanimously nominate their own government for the honor."*
**Reginald Dale, *International Herald Tribune*, 4/6/1993**

*"Britain's rail network is now one of the most unreliable, slowest and costliest in Europe."*
**_The Economist_, 12/3/1994**

# Infrawhat?

There can be no better and more objective index of a country's health than the state of its infrastructure.

I watch the local news on British TV in the mornings just to find out how many burst water mains are reported that day. Somehow it seems symptomatic of things generally (for some reason burst gas mains don't make the headlines in the same way, presumably because gas, unlike water, doesn't block roads).

Thanks to the British Road Federation and the petroleum lobbies, roads have become essential to all those people who commute by car. The rest go by rail, their challenge being frozen points, leaves on the line or 'the wrong sort of snow'. I have never known a European country with such a folkloric infrastructure.

Yet any sensible English person knows full well that an efficient infrastructure helps cope with the business of living, even if it messes up the quality of life a bit.

*'The British team can't get going.
Apparently it's the wrong sort of snow'.*

The history of Britain since the Industrial Revolution is a record of an inconsequential and erratic approach to the country's transportation systems. Once upon a time there was coastal shipping, then there were the inland canals. Both were overtaken by the train. Then came the trams. The automobile and petroleum lobbies saw to it that the tramway systems were ritually sacrificed in all British cities after 1945, precisely at a time when many Continental countries saw them as the best long-term solution to inner city public transport.

The railway infrastructure, which had been pioneered with so much effort and expense only one hundred years before, was then made the object of benign, maybe malign, indifference and neglect. The result today is that Britain has a crumbling and half abandoned network – abandoned both to weeds and to private investors – while France enters the 21st century with a state-owned system and TGVs.

London's tubes are the most decrepit and expensive of any of Europe's capital city underground systems. While England cobbles up, France uses a visionary mix of state grants, local government activism, levies on local business and civic initiative to boost public transport and curb the car. As an example, Lille replaced its entire tramway fleet in mid-1994 and is busy extending its metro. Meanwhile Birmingham, the UK's second largest conurbation, pleads desperately and despairingly for government funding for a single high-speed rail line. Realism on the Continent, doctrinaire attitudes at home – it used to be the other way round.

I am left feeling that we English are committed to not taking anything too seriously, not even the most basic components of an effective society. Even the road system is showing increasing signs of strain – not surprisingly since it carries twice as many cars per kilometre (or per mile, come to that) as France or Belgium.

As a people who are supposed to hate a doctrinaire approach to anything, we have excelled ourselves on this particular and very vital issue.

The official neglect of and prevarication over the railway system would put to shame the government of any industrialised nation with the exception of the United States, which has done no better. Consider the saga of the London-Channel Tunnel link!

The country now has the infrastructure it did not deserve. Communities have seen their umbilical cords cut, with the closing of branch lines, and inadequate road links offered in their place. Government has sabotaged one of its greatest assets and derailed communities and individuals in the process.

According to *Rail Business Report*, Britain continues to invest less in its rail network per kilometre of track than any well-to-do European country but Finland. In fact, the country's per capita investment in railways is currently less than one-third of the European average.

Since we have landed on the subject of the dogmatism of a people who are reputedly (dare I say almost dogmatically?) opposed to any form of dogmatism, let me point out another quirk from recent history.

Post-war Germany emerged from the ruins determined to redeem itself by the assiduous application of new ideas and techniques. The irony is that many of the initiatives that resulted first took shape in the heads and hearts of English people working in an occupiers' organisation known as the Control Commission. These ideas and techniques included consolidated trades unions, the 'additional member system' (comparable to proportional representation), two-tier management structures with worker participation, *Der Spiegel*, the revitalisation of VW, the *Grüne Welle* ('green waves') traffic control system, even a federal constitution.

All these ideas were spurned at home, in Britain. Our young Turks were fully at liberty to try them out on hapless foreigners, but the possibility that they might be allowed to challenge the traditions of centuries in the Dear Old Country itself was unthinkable. So Germany benefited and Britain continued on its own aimless way.

Britain has also churlishly refused to acknowledge the role of the German locomotive in keeping the European train on the move with the English carriage bringing up the rear. With the additional load of reunification, the German effort vastly outmatches the British contribution – even with North Sea oil thrown in for free.

Infrastructure is not just railways and motorways of course. It extends to other vital areas of life. Burst water mains are only one of the manifestations of a decrepit water system. Others are river pollution, the curious habit of locating sewage farms on the coast (a seemingly good idea, but one unlikely to enhance the beauty of the surroundings) and the direct discharge of untreated effluent into the ocean (a dirty habit guaranteed to foul the environment, hence Britain's lingering reputation for filthy beaches).

Then there is the business of holes in the ground. The glass recycling industry made valiant efforts to promote its

## Underground and underprepared

One of the odd things about the Channel Tunnel is that, rather than bringing Europeans closer together, it seems to be setting them further apart. It started before even the first sod was turned: "The French spent money and planned before they began", said a Eurotunnel executive at the time. "The British just walked on to the site and started up."

As French management expert Jean-Louis Barsoux has said in another context, "the French like to be able to see the end of the tunnel before they enter it."

The cult of walking on site underprepared – apart from a knack for responding pragmatically to circumstances – is a peculiarly English phenomenon. It may be seen as a stereotype, but it has some substance and is based on observation. Another stereotype, with substance and prejudice, is evident in the words of a member of the British drilling team when the two met in the middle: "We've must have broken through. There's a whiff of garlic in the air."

Throughout the development of this high-speed rail link between the Anglo-Saxon and the Latin world, differences of attitude have been dramatic. While the British procrastinated and examined their consciences, the French went into action. Their realism, helped along by the usual dose of government dirigism, produced high-speed results. Local administrators fell over one another to make sure that the track ran through their constituency and not the one next door – in complete contrast to the gentry of 'the Garden of England', who did everything possible to ensure that the track went through somebody else's back garden.

In fairness to the French, some of them still put quality of life first. The administrators of one *commune* on the proposed route did everything possible to frustrate the planners' intentions. With Gallic ingenuity, they bought a strategic plot of land and sold it in one-square-meter lots to people in places like Hawaii and Hong Kong, creating a legal web that not even the French government would have been able to unravel. Not content with this, the mayor gave instructions, in the event of his death, to have his remains buried on site. With all the excitement he had a heart attack and died. But French dirigism had the last word: the planners expropriated land alongside the plot and rerouted the line.

Even the styling and layout of the high-speed trains for the Eurotunnel link has stimulated cultural conflict. *The International Herald Tribune* reports how "the British favored a stylized replica of the classic Orient Express; the Belgians wanted the interior divided into traditional six-person compartments; the French wanted open airline-style seating. After months of discord, a gentleman's agreement was reached. The British would design the exterior, the Belgians would do the toilets and the baggage compartments and the French would handle the rest." As usual the British and the Belgians compromised – and the French won.

With the Tunnel now operational, these cultural differences are finally earning recognition. Nobody seems particularly concerned that, whereas the information displays at the French end of the Tunnel are uncompromisingly futuristic, the ones at the British end are unrepentently nostalgic. And as Eurotunnel's director of human resources, Yves-Noel Derenne, acknowledged in a recent interview, "for a team in the UK a uniform is important. In France, you belong to the team, but you don't want to be seen to belong."

Even the fact that a TGV fell into a foxhole on the outskirts of Lille didn't alarm the English for once – although some French people had grounds for momentary alarm when the train derailed at 300kph but stayed upright (another triumph for French technology). English visions of rabid foxes entering the UK via a Tunnel already well defended with anti-rabid-fox-fences were dispelled when it became known that the 'foxhole' was a WWI trench, and maybe even a British one at that.

Bottle Bank scheme but, despite the typical English flair for showmanship and self-promotion, could not achieve anything like the return rate recorded by Continental countries. When asked why this was, a representative for the industry succinctly replied: "there are too many holes in the ground".

Evidently holes in the ground continue to be a distinctly English problem: there seem to be more and more of them around. Ordinary people are having to fight to prevent the despoliation of their countryside by euphemistically dubbed 'landfills' and by open-cast mining – a hurried expedient to meet the shortfall in power-station coal caused by premature and often brutal pit closures.

If this goes on, internal erosion of this tight little island may become as big a threat as erosion from the sea. Only recently Frederick Forsyth, author of Day of the Jackel, felt obliged to pitch in for the benefit of a Hertfordshire community threatened by a sandpit-turned-rubbish-tip. High drama!

The fact that we English have an essentially no-nonsense attitude towards our bodies does not explain government neglect of the health service, which Sir Raymond Hoffenberg described in mid-1994 as "systematically eroded by underfunding". No continental country west of the old Iron Curtain can offer such run-down hospitals, with such demoralised and defeated staff, as Britain.

And to cap all these things, in the words of Philippe Daudy who is a friendly but acute observer of the English scene, "in the last fifty years there has been little town planning worthy of the name." In fact, when the disastrous Canary Wharf project was mooted, the government went out of its way to lift planning controls.

A study published by the Council for the Protection of Rural England in 1993 41 shows that, between 1945 and 1990, 705,000 hectares of rural land – an area greater than that of Greater London, Hertfordshire and Oxfordshire combined – were lost to urban uses of various kinds.

Once urbanised, English hectares (ex-acres) tend to become dirty and undistinguished. Local government, what's left of it, is demoralised and central government won't cough up. The dirt is not confined to provincial cities either. In his book *Neither Here Nor There*[42] American journalist Bill Bryson lets drop the fact – it seems it was a fact in 1991 – that Paris spends £58 a year a head on street-cleaning compared with London's £17 a head. He actually called England a kind of nation-state equivalent of Woolworth's. I say, old chap!

At this rate, any hope of turning the island into a theme park with eccentric lords, straw-chewing yokels and tweedy Misses Marples – to the relief of the inhabitants and the delight of foreigners – will have to be abandoned.

*"In the European Community, Britain's government insists on subsidiarity... At home, it does nothing of the sort."*

**The Economist, 14/8/1993**

*"Britain is locked into a vicious circle: the reduced powers of local authorities mean unimpressive councillors are elected by a few ill-informed voters, which helps to justify a further reduction in local-authority powers."*

**The Economist, 7/5/1994**

*"While politicians fiercely defend the sovereignty of parliament, their citizens are already having to look outside Britain for the defence of their basic freedoms."*

**Anthony Sampson, The Essential Anatomy of Britain**

*"The history of Europe since World War II is largely the tale of its division by British pride and obstinacy."*

**John W Holmes, World Peace Foundation**

*"What has emerged in shop floor behaviour through fear and anxiety is much greater than I think could have been secured by more cooperative methods."*

**Nigel Lawson, Tory Chancellor**

*"The political item on the reform agenda ought to be British democracy. It has suffered in various ways: from Whitehall's passion for secrecy, from the squeeze on local government and the rise of an unelected quangocracy, from the transfers of powers to Brussels. Democratic reform was a crusade for Lady Thatcher – but only in Eastern Europe, not at home."*

**The Economist, 31/7/1993**

*"We are the most secretive of any democratic society – that goes without saying."*

**Lord McGregor, Chairman of the Press Complaints
Commission, January 1993**

*"To look at Britain you would not believe that anyone was in charge."*

**Michael Thompson-Noel, Financial Times, 2/7/1994**

# Fudge and humbug

In his book *Rule Britannia* published in 1981[43], James Bellini proffered the 'Norman conspiracy' theory:

"In the 1080s, some nine centuries ago, William the Conqueror ordered a study of his newly acquired territory. The picture that emerged from the Domesday Survey of 1086 was of a strictly ordered society in which a ladder of privilege, rank, status, wealth, power and subservience was clearly defined.

"In the nine centuries that have elapsed since..., only the words have changed in this description of Britain's condition... Two hundred years of industry can now be seen only as the means of creating a new aristocracy to enrich and extend the aristocracy of old landed wealth."

This conspiracy theory is an intriguing one (there is a similar theory that the US is masterminded by a political elite descended from families that, appropriately, inherited their prerogatives from the English). The aristocracy of old landed wealth, descended from the Normans, is as tangible as it ever was. Despite the government's refusal to introduce a public register of land ownership – yet another doctrinaire stance that defies commonsense – there is evidence that the ten biggest landowners own over 1.5 million acres between them and that concentration of ownership extends much further than this.

The conspiracy theory postulates that this 'aristocracy of old landed wealth' has imposed its value system on the rest of society through something resembling a long-term brainwashing process. Back in 1863 Richard Cobden said that "manufacturers and merchants as a rule seem only to desire riches that they may be enabled to prostrate themselves at the feet of feudalism" and then asked "how is this to end?".

George Orwell elaborated the theme in his book *The Lion and the Unicorn*[44], written in 1941, when he said: "After

111

1832 the old land-owning aristocracy steadily lost power, but instead of disappearing or becoming a fossil they simply intermarried with the merchants, manufacturers and financiers who had replaced them, and soon turned them into accurate copies of themselves. The wealthy shipowner or cotton-miller set up for himself an alibi as a country gentleman, while his sons learned the right mannerisms at public schools which had been designed for just that purpose".

Even more recently, in *Millenium*, Francis Kinsman said much the same thing: "Our class system makes for a safe feudal society, just as it does for Japan; but instead of the mainspring of this feudalism being group achievement and an economic conquest almost military in its ruthlessness, our British feudalism is primarily orientated towards the maintenance of a comfortable status quo. The British establishment is change averse, its main aim being to keep things bobbing along more or less as they are until retirement, after which somebody else can sort out the mess."

"The successful American businessman who makes five million", Kinsman continued, "starts planning to turn it into 50 million; the successful British businessman who makes five million starts planning to turn it into a Georgian manor house on the Test. Ostentatious success is ungentlemanly and suspect *per se*; acceptable success entails joining the same old clubs rather than founding new ones." Yes, sir!

One of my UK passport-holding friends is a professional student of the English way of life: he runs a social research company. He believes in the conspiracy theory and reckons that English society ultimately ranges a 'Norman' elite against

Anglo-Saxon serfs. His theory even accommodates the burgeoning of the service economy: "the elite welcomes this trend because it keeps the serfs servile and minimises the threat from an industrial lobby."

He may have something there, though the idea is not very fair to the Normans, even if it is fair to the establishment today – aided or not, depending on your point of view, by the National Trust. The Normans, after all, accepted merit in its own right and they did, incidentally, bring that most beautiful of architectural styles, the Romanesque, to England.

"Unlike most other European countries", my sociologist friend continues, "we have an alliance between land and money rather than between money and industry. This structure is much more important than the urban-rural division. Progress in solving our problems is most unlikely unless we can bring about a complete divorce between land and money, thus freeing the money to go into industry. I also believe that this process will have to start right at the top, which is why I question the role of the monarchy."

The conspiracy plot thickens and the cast gets bigger – but the theory can be elaborated further. There has always been a sentimental attachment to rural values and an antagonism toward industrial ones at all levels of English society. It found its voice in the 'Condition of England' novels of Victorian times, which looked back to a golden age that supposedly predated the Industrial Revolution.

In 1982, Christopher Lorenz wrote in the *Financial Times* about "the deep-rooted attraction to rural values, and antipathy towards industrial ones, which has been bred into most middle-class English men and women for over a century by the educational system and by the very structure of society."

A foreign observer, Ralf Dahrendorf, former director of the London School of Economics, appeared to be thinking along the same lines when he said: "The essentially static views of the old British upper class have won the day in Britain. They have spread, first to the working class, then to the middle class, or perhaps the other way round. But they have not been diluted, let alone replaced, by the ambitions and achievements of the industrial middle class".

Whatever we may conclude, and whether the Normans are guilty or not, England is in the hands of an in-group – more exactly a group of in-groups – with mutually supporting and supportive interests.

Of course in this respect the country is no different from other European countries: even the destinies of apparently democratic and even-handed societies like Sweden and the Netherlands are ultimately in the hands of a privileged few.

But it is not the existence of this English elite, inevitable as it is, that troubles me. It is the criteria these people apply to the way the country is run and where it is going, and ultimately their mindless acceptance of historical values. Of course this is the tribute they have to pay for joining or being part of this group of in-groups, the establishment.

This deeply entrenched habit bodes ill for England if, in the process of protecting and furthering its interests, the establishment continues to practice the dilatoriness, fudge and obfuscation that has been its hallmark for decades.

HM Government uses the principle of royal prerogative and the absence of a written constitution and bill of rights to exercise an enormous degree of unaccountable power and privilege relative to other European countries. With the con-

*As a historic example of English fudge and humbug, I offer the following report from a leading British financial paper, late-1967:*

# Vote of Thanks

In proposing a vote of thanks to the chairman, directors and all members of the [name of company] organization, Sir [name of person] said:

"Mr Chairman, may I claim the privilege, as a very sincere admirer of [name of company], to say a few words. We have heard from you, Sir, a major address this morning which has covered a huge range and it has brought home to us what a very important organization [name of company] is and what a heavy responsibility rests on your shoulders, Sir, and on those of your colleagues.

You have had some bitter pills to swallow during the last eight months and we would have sympathized if you had indulged in polemics when you reported to us the disappointments involved in the [name of cancelled project] and [name of compromised project] and [name of disbanded company]. You have chosen instead to use sober language and you have reported to us in very carefully chosen words; and this did not detract at all from the impact that you made on us. Your message came through loud and clear, Sir – loud and clear.

May I say how much we admired the dignity with which you have suffered these blows. With other people there may have been a bit of snivelling, but not with you, Sir, no jobbing backwards. Instead of that – an immediate search of how best to use the resources of the company which are going to be released. This is free enterprise at its best. No dwelling on the past; willingness to change and looking into the future, and that is how we want to carry on.

May I also say how much we welcome what you have had to say about the chance that you were going to give to the young in [name of company], and particularly the phrase which you used. 'They will assume complete responsibility, above all, for the profit which they contribute to the group.' I am convinced that efficiency and therefore the future of our country must rest on the profit motive. We welcome, therefore, the chance that you are going to give to the young people of your company to show what they are made of.

Sir, while I am standing on my feet, may I thank you and [name of company] for all the support that you have given to me during my term of office as President of the Federation [name of federation]; and perhaps you will just allow me to mention particularly Sir [name of person] who, amongst all his duties, has given me so much help and so much of his great ability and great wisdom.

Finally, Sir, may I express, on behalf of all the members here, our thanks for all you personally have done for us in the past and to express the confidence of the meeting in you and in your colleagues to look after our investments in the future and to maintain the name of [name of company] as a symbol of efficiency."

The proposal was carried with acclamation.

**NB1:**

This is not a parody, but an authentic reproduction of a newspaper report, names omitted. It appeared in late-1967, when I was leaving the UK, as it turned out, for good. I took it as a memento.

**NB2:**

The company, which is no longer a symbol of efficiency, swallowed some more bitter pills later on... and, of course, the young were given no chance.

nivance of the monarchy, it hands out largesse, titles, ministerships, peerages and the like to those who can be expected not to rock the boat. It is now aiming to constrain members of the underclass and other social undesirables with the Criminal Justice and Public Order Bill.

The greatest obfuscation is the smokescreen of 'parliamentary democracy', a device used by Ministers to justify almost anything, including the refusal to let people decide for themselves. In the words of *The Economist*, "Britain has a system of parliamentary absolutism which is centralised and unbalanced to a remarkable degree... The truth is that the British system, which its admirers laud as being peculiarly flexible and responsive, is rigid and slow to adapt to outside change."[45]

Not only is the system rigid and slow to adapt, it is excessively secretive. Indeed government even shows a gift for fudging the 'official' figures.

I am not suggesting we go as far as Sweden, where open government extends to citizens looking at the Prime Minister's mail. But we might make some concessions to greater transparency, to use that awful Continental word. Even little Belgium acknowledges the principle that "everyone has the right to consult any document produced by the administration and to obtain a copy".

In Britain, about the only direct evidence the voter has of what is going on is the televised proceedings of the Lower House. To judge from these, he or she is putting the country's future in the hands of a bunch of loudmouthed and irresponsible schoolboys and girls. The yaroo mentality is in stark contrast to the formal monologues of Continental 'theatre-in-the-round' assemblies' which lack the theatre! Yet much of the real decision-making rests with special committees or with the parliamentary lobbies and interest groups, the most sophisticated of any member-state of the European Union.

Cyril Northcote Parkinson, the creator of Parkinson's Law, said of Westminster that "the British [his choice of words, and in this case he's right], being brought up on team games, enter their House of Commons in the spirit of those who would rather be doing something else. If they cannot be playing golf or tennis, they can at least pretend that politics is a game with very similar rules." They certainly don't seem to be taking things very seriously – even if some of them, particularly those on the opposition benches, are very serious indeed.

The moral outrage demonstrated by some backbencher MPs – occasionally from the Loony Left but more often from the Ridiculous Right – classes as pure theatre in the best, or worst, Westminster tradition.

But the greatest insult is that government pretends this is democracy in practice and, in response to suggestions that voters' interests are poorly represented, points accusingly at Brussels – blithely ignoring the fact that they are the ones who, through the mechanism of the Council of Ministers, are making the ultimate decisions there too.

In reality, the democratic deficit between Westminster and the constituencies is far greater than the one between Brussels and Westminster. It is bizarrely appropriate that the phrase used to describe the process of national elections is 'to go to the country', the suggestion being that only the Westminster-Whitehall axis features on the political map of Britain in the years between.

On top of the distortions of the first-past-the-post system – which such balkanised political communities as Italy find seductive – and the slavishness of so-called constituency representatives to party whips, the role of local government has been viciously savaged.

As *The Economist* remarked in May 1994[46], "outside authoritarian regimes, it is hard to name any country in the world where local government is so circumscribed as in Britain." Talk about 'subsidiarity'!

The English cry louder about subsidiarity than anyone else, yet fail to practise it in their own country – and not just with regard to the aspirations of the Scots and the Welsh. Not even the French can muster such Pavlovian responses as the English do, positively, to words like 'sovereignty' and 'subsidiarity' and, negatively, to a word like 'federalism' (the 'F-word').

On the matter of sovereignty, as Samuel Brittan has said, "the latter has already been eroded ... by Britain's own elective dictatorship". To which I would add that squeals about losing sovereignty to an independent European Union central bank, when the Bank of England has for too long been a tool of short-term government policy far removed from the interests of the electorate, smack of total humbug.

Happily there are signs that this standard of double-think is now being discredited. Yet there are people who still argue that making the Bank of England independent will weaken parliamentary accountability. What parliamentary accountability?

Things are not helped by the latest fashion for putting responsibility for swathes of social activity in the hands of executive agencies. The terms of reference, vis-a-vis the electorate, of this new generation of quangos are often ill-defined or non-existent. Similar organisations on the Continent have their duties laid down by statute. Quangos also provide a wonderful source of jobs for the boys. Some 10,000 appointments are made every year yet significantly, in 1992, only 24 of these were advertised!

*The Economist* also challenges claims to open government: "Britain's government is notoriously closed. There is none of the public debate on policy that characterises Scandinavian and American government. There is no freedom-of-information law, such as exists in Denmark, Holland and France, as well as in the United States, Canada and Australia." And the article adds, fairly, "Mr Major may be trying hard, but the culture takes some changing." And how!

A typical example is the government's attitude to the creation of a land register, a seemingly reasonable proposition. Here, the fudge and humbug is laid on really thick. Whitehall insists that such an initiative would infringe the Data Protection Act, yet the government itself switches information through its data network from one agency to the other without the slightest compunction. Try to find out what authority this practice is based on and the shutters come down. It seems that, in the matter of who has right of access to information and who doesn't, English empiricism is carried to the limit.

However hard Mr Major or his successors try, changing the culture will no longer solve things on its own. The credibility gap – another deficit – is now so great that the establishment has lost the confidence of its constituents. An ICM poll taken in late-1993[47] showed that the civil service was trusted by only 21% of the public, parliament by only 13% and the government by only 11%!

But hands up those who think the culture can, or should be, be changed? I wonder how many. And with so much inertia in English society, it's a wonder there are still people around who find it necessary to put the clock back...

In the concluding chapter of his book, James Bellini says: "No society in the western world has yet attempted to rediscover 'the world we have lost'. Put to the popular vote, none would choose to." In the case of the English, I'm not so sure.

Trying to put the clock back is a fool's pursuit, blindly resisting progress no better. Pretending that we can go on in the same old way when the world is changing dramatically all around us is suicide. But we are right to protect the best of what we have.

Like what's left of our natural heritage. On his way round Britain, Paul Theroux followed the dramatically beautiful coastline of Cornwall. Not long ago a London entrepreneur's plan to develop a spot on the south Cornish coast ran into fierce local opposition. When the locals demonstrated on his site, the developer shouted that they were obviously not interested in progress. "Go back to England and make your mess!", was the reply.

The following night the demonstrators left a sign on the site: "Tu has tre Sawsnek Coth" or, in Sassenach, "take yourselves homewards Anglo-Saxons!" They forgot the Normans!

*"The United Kingdom may be drifting further and further away from the continent – and from the EU. Perhaps it should consider joining the North American Free Trade Agreement?"*  **Strategy Weekly, 13/7/1994**

*"In a quiet way the British were hopeful, and because in the cycle of ruin and renewal there had been so much ruin, they were glad to be still holding on – that was the national mood – hard put to explain their survival. The British seemed to me to be people forever standing on a crumbling coast and scanning the horizon. So I had done the right thing in traveling the coast, and instead of looking out to sea, I had looked inland."*

**Paul Theroux, *The Kingdom by the Sea*, 1982**

*"When Armageddon arrives, the English will be there with (depending on class) their chipped mugs of tea and their bangers, or their champagne as cool as their crustless cucumber sandwiches, talking rainfall statistics."*

**The Mid-Atlantic Companion**

*"I have.. even developed a certain admiration for this nation which takes so much pleasure in analysing its own decline – too much, in fact, to be taken seriously."*

**French journalist Denis Brulet**

*"The insularity of the English, their refusal to take foreigners seriously, is a folly that has to be paid for very heavily from time to time."*

**George Orwell, *The Lion and the Unicorn***

*"Britain will resemble the orchestra at the end of one of the Marx Brothers' films, playing sublimely but unaware that it was drifting out to sea."*

**Sir Roy Denman, *International Herald Tribune*, 2/2/1993**

*"I am American bred,*
*I have seen much to hate here – much to forgive,*
*But in a world (without Englishmen),*
*I do not wish to live."*  **Alice Duer Miller, *The White Cliffs***

124

# So who's fooling whom?

So what do we do about the Dear Old Country (DOC)?

It is difficult to trust official statistics. After all, the government has doubts about its own balance of trade estimates, a healthy scepticism shared by the public at large. But some indicators are difficult to ignore.

One of them is the OECD's estimates of the annual average increase in GDP. In the four years 1989-93, Britain recorded the lowest growth of any of the twelve member states of the European Union: 0.9%. In terms of absolute per capita GDP, the country now ranks No 8 behind Italy and the Netherlands. In fact, in the last 15 years, the UK has had the lowest growth rate of any industrialised country in the world. Not even the massive and not-to-be-repeated inflows from North Sea oil and privatisations have changed the picture.

For a nation which used to pride itself on its prosperity and economic power, this is a sorry state of affairs. Qualms about the distribution of what prosperity there is do not add to confidence. The record looks bad.

To quote a *Guardian* editorial of May 1994, "the Second World War made us too proud, disabled our capacity for self-criticism and prevented us from seeing where our future interests lay. The myth that we had stood alone and triumphed fed a half-century of misplaced complacency about British power and prestige, for which we are now paying the price."

Today, the DOC has little power economically or politically, so we fabricate prestige on the basis of sentimental and ultrafragile concepts like 'the balance of power' and 'the special relationship'. As a Tory MP was heard to say recently to one of his German counterparts: "My dear chap, it has been Britain's role over the past 200 years to maintain the balance of power in Europe, and we've certainly no intention of giving up that role now." Is that the intention behind all the government's European chicanery?

As for the 'special relationship', ironically this has suffered more at the hands of Tory Eurosceptics than at those of anyone else. As somebody has said, I think it was Philippe Daudy, we would sooner be second to the United States than first in Europe. Little chance of either now.

Of course, if we prefer to argue that the much-lauded English quality of life takes absolute precedence over prosperity, we may be happy being bottom of the league. But the record looks dubious here too.

In early-1994 the Stockholm Environment Institute developed an Index of Sustainable Economic Welfare (ISEW) [48] for the UK which, in addition to GNP, factored in measures of the economic aspects of resource depletion and long-term environmental damage. This showed that, while per capita GNP had grown by 35% in the years 1974-1990, per capita ISEW had declined by over half. An uncomfortable conclusion for a country supposedly dedicated to this quality of life!

Deteriorating quality of life may also help explain why, since WWII, people of all classes and backgrounds have been voting with their feet – tradespeople and shopfloor technicians to Australia and South Africa, scientists to the USA, frustrated executives to Europe. About one million people of all ages emigrated from the DOC in the five years to 1990 though, paradoxically, the country switched from a steady net emigration flow to net immigration in 1987. Even so, a *Daily Telegraph* opinion poll in 1993 found that 49% of respondents would still prefer to live abroad if they could.

So what is happening? In the opinion of the historian Theodore Zeldin, the English are losing their ability to complain and whatever capacity they may have had to revolt. They are, it seems, escaping inside themselves – into humour, into TV and other diversions and sadly, in some cases, into xenophobia.

A British expatriate manager working with a major international services corporation finds that his fellow-countryfolk are the most resistant of all European nationalities to ideas from outside. He talks of "Fortress Britain" and attributes their resistance largely to a loss of self-esteem, as a community rather than as individuals, and to the resulting mood of defensiveness.

Even back in 1982, Paul Theroux sensed that all was not well (curiously he always uses the past tense in his book, which makes me wonder whether he views the DOC as a has-been or thinks that change is in the air?): "Going to the coast was as far as they could comfortably go. It was the poor person's way of going abroad – standing at the seaside and staring at the ocean. It took a little imagination. I believed that these people were fantasizing that they were over there on the watery horizon, at sea. Most people on the Promenade walked with their faces averted from the land. Perhaps another of their coastal pleasures was being able to turn their backs on Britain. I seldom saw anyone with his back turned to the sea (it was the rarest posture on the coast). Most people looked seaward with anxious hopeful faces, as if they had just left their native land."

A bit far-fetched? I wonder... It seems that a couple by the name of Shaw have named their daughter 'Bythesee'. The Channel and the oceans loom large in the English folk psyche!

Will the last person to leave England please turn out the lights?

I wonder where and why the English, a people with so many qualities, have gone so wrong? They are an essentially kindly people and Britain used to be a caring society. The first hospices for the dying were British, not Swiss or Swedish. The NHS pioneered European standards of responsibility toward public health care.

As a people the English are consensus-oriented, despite the ding-dong antics of public life. As individuals, in the eyes and estimation of foreigners, they stand out for their "docility" (Philippe Daudy), their "kindness" (Lynn Payer), their "tolerance" (Paul Theroux), their "gentleness" (George Orwell). Tolerance, interpreted also as "fair play" by Continentals, though not always respected by the English, is the leitmotif of the island culture.

Lynn Payer says that British doctors are "more sensitive to the 'soft' side effects that may affect a patient's quality of life more than the hard ones" (ah, that quality of life again!). Is it possible that Mrs T, riding on the wave of a revulsion against both social privilege and state excesses, fundamentally misread the English psyche?

On the one hand, we see an independently minded, ambitious, almost swashbuckling spirit in English society. On the other, there is a sense of caring, of genuinely wanting to be fair, an appreciation of other things in life than just money or success – after all there are, as I have conceded throughout, many people who think preservation of quality of life is what it is all about.

They may be right, provided their concerns are not just a defensive reflex when faced with the country's inability to keep up with the rest of the world. But, whatever the reality, Mrs T obviously got only half the picture.

The underlying dilemma – individual achievement versus social consensus – has been posed in simplistic, binary

**THE BRITISH CHARACTER**

A TENDENCY TO THINK THINGS NOT SO GOOD AS THEY USED TO BE

terms. Yet there is a middle ground, where both have their place. Sadly this middle ground is occupied by ceremonial, class consciousness and, increasingly, centralisation.

English people are perfectly entitled to want to stick to their traditions and let the rest of the world go hang. But administrative centralisation is in reality hastening the erosion of traditional values and ways of life. Helped on its way by gentrification and divisiveness – rather than real divisions! – in a society which used to practice a curious but genuine form of fellow-feeling and reciprocity, the process is obliterating old communities and allegiances.

By the standards of many Continental societies, family life has almost ceased to exist in Britain. The parent/child relationship is, all too often, the 'shut-up-and-don't-ask-questions' attitude of the working class or the jollying-along approach of the upwardly mobile middle classes. You sometimes need to be a mindreader to guess there's any parental love involved.

The most distressing thing of all is what looks suspiciously like a wanton if half-conscious waste of so much human talent. Many English people have great creative potential, uninhibited by Uncertainty Avoidance, but their in-built nonchalance makes them negligent of these talents.

Paul Theroux: "They could be deeply dismissive and self-critical... But being self-critical in this way was also a tactic for remaining ineffectual. It was surrender." And this is not just because we have the unusual gift of being able to laugh at ourselves! In the words of Peter Collett, "the use of humour in adversity is central to the English character – some would say that it is what defines Englishness."

To which I would add the gift of amateurism: it is not a coincidence that our vocabulary provides for the concept of 'the gifted amateur'. Yet, as an academic who studies the English character reminded me the other day, there are amateurs and amateurs: "the gifted ones are an asset, but the others are a serious liability!"

Added to which the gift of amateurism looks increasingly like an inability to cope, resulting in a permanent state of muddle. In the words of an Anglo-Irish friend, "the English seem to need disasters before they sort themselves out."

But the real problem – in case I have not made myself clear – is that, in the process of coping with life, we have unwittingly and paradoxically become doctrinaire. This, allied with disillusionment about party politics, the most doctrinaire segment of English society, may help explain another island phenomenon: the proliferation of special-interest and activist groups like Friends of the Earth, the Animal Liberation Front, the Child Poverty Action Group, the Donga

132

Tribe and so on (in parenthesis, the Royal Society for the Protection of Birds now counts more members than the three main political parties together!).

At many levels of English society, we think in almost manichaean terms, seeing everything in black and white. It's not a question of Tory versus Labour, Europe versus 'the special relationship', nationalisation versus privatisation. The world is more subtle than that. How have we become such a doctrinaire people when our instinct is to be so pragmatic?

It looks to me as if we need a detoxification cure. In fact, to use an infamous phrase in a different context, why don't we go back to basics? If we English are an empirical people – and there's plenty of evidence to that effect – we have the enormous advantage of being free of the logical formalism of other European cultures. As individuals, we can draw on our personal experiences and extrapolate them in any way we think fit. We have a creative potential that is, for all sorts of reasons originating within our society, sadly misdirected.

As an American journalist said to me when I was putting the finishing touches to this book, "when Britons understand the world beyond their island, and move comfortably in that world, they can be formidably effective".

Uninhibited by the Strong Uncertainty Avoidance of others, our free-wheeling creativity comes so naturally that we are, more often than not, unaware of this gift. No wonder we English are perplexing.

And our fellow Europeans are perplexed. Many voice their disappointment and bewilderment at the fact that Britain

133

is mentally and morally absent from the centre of the action – except, more often than not, in a disruptive mode. They do not expect consensus, but they do hope for a more positive

contribution from us in building a better future. And, in the words of a publication I have cited frequently in this book, "many of them believe Britain would win more arguments if it pushed its way to the heart of the negotiations, rather than, as so often, carp on the sidelines." [49]

Happily some British youth – at least those that have the good fortune and the opportunity to express themselves on the subject – seem to dissociate themselves from the reticences and hangups of their elders. So there is hope, even if the government has decided to put more, rather than less, emphasis on British history in the National Curriculum. Like young people throughout Europe, this new generation has the opportunity to form its own opinions – through travelling, through intermingling with other nationalities and, it has to be said, by learning from the dismal record of our country over recent years.

Official data released in 1994 show that more and more young people are choosing to stay in the educational system after the age of 16 and, in many cases, plan to go on to university. This is encouraging. If more people can articulate what they think is wrong, the greater the chance the establishment will act to put things right. But will it?

Not if we are to believe George Orwell who, in *The Lion and the Unicorn*, said of the ruling classes that "there was only one escape for them – into stupidity. They could keep society in its existing shape only by being unable to grasp that any improvement was possible. Difficult though this was, they achieved it, largely by fixing their eyes on the past and refusing to notice the changes that were going on around them".

Many of the developments foreseen in his book, written in 1941, failed to materialise. Yet his analysis of that England bears an uncanny resemblance to the country today, suggesting that things have hardly changed in the meantime.

"England is not the jewelled isle of Shakespeare's much-quoted message, nor is it the inferno depicted by Dr Goebbels. More than either it resembles a family, with not many black sheep in it but with all its cupboards bursting with skeletons. It has rich relations who have to be kow-towed to and poor relations who are horribly sat upon, and there is a deep conspiracy of silence about the source of the family income. It is a family in which the young are generally thwarted and most of the power is in the hands of irresponsible uncles and bed-ridden aunts. Still, it is a family. It has its private language and its common memories, and at the approach of an enemy it closes its ranks. A family with the wrong members in control – that, perhaps, is as near as one can come to describing England in a phrase."

In conclusion, a parody of John Betjeman's memorable lines:

*"Think of what our nation stands for,*
*Books from Boots and country lanes,*
*Free speech, free passes, class distinction,*
*Democracy and proper drains"*

> **Think of what a mess we've got in,**
> **Traffic jams, burst water mains,**
> **Free love, free lunches, class distinction,**
> **Autocracy and tacky trains**

We still have class distinction!

# BIBLIOGRAPHY

1   Eurobarometer 40. Brussels: Surveys Research Unit, European Commission, December 1993.

2   Daninos, Pierre. The Notebooks of Major Thompson. London: Atheneum Macmillan, 1982.

3   Daudy, Philippe. Les Anglais: Portrait of a People. London: Headline Book Publishing, 1992.

4   Mikes, George. How to be an Alien. London: Penguin Books, 1966.

5   Payer, Lynn. Medicine and Culture. London: Gollancz, 1990.

6   Hofstede, Geert. Cultures and Organizations. London: McGraw-Hill Book Company, 1991.

7   The European, 15-21/7/1994, "Eccentric souls find the key to longer life".

8   Theroux, Paul. The Kingdom by the Sea: a Journey around Great Britain. New York: Washington Square Press, 1983.

9   Collett, Peter. Foreign Bodies. London, Simon & Schuster, 1993.

10  Orwell, George. Politics and the English Language, 1946.

11  International Herald Tribune, 2/2/1994, "Read All About It – Good Old Brits vs. the Wicked Continent".

12  International Herald Tribune, 25/2/1993, "Britain: Demoralized, Let Down by Mediocre Elites".

13  Lewis, Flora. Europe: a Tapestry of Nations. New York: Touchstone, 1987.

14  St George, Andrew. The Descent of Manners. London: Chatto & Windus, 1993.

15  Mikes, George. How to be a Brit. London: Penguin, 1984.

16  MORI for Sunday Express, August 1991.

17  Zeldin, Theodore. The French. London: Collins Harvill, 1983.

18  Powell, Chris. Humour in Society: Resistance and Control. Basingstoke: Macmillan, 1988.

19  Riddell, Peter. The Thatcher Decade: How Britain has changed during the 1980s. Oxford: Basil Blackwell, 1989.

20  The Low Pay Unit, 1994.

21  Smith, David. North and South. London: Penguin Books, 1994.

22  The Economist, 4/6/1994, "The unhealthy poor".

23  Wilkinson, Richard. Unfair Shares. Ilford: Barnardo's, 1994.

24  The Economist, 20/11/1993, "The basic issue".

25  Commission on Social Justice, July 1993.

26  The Basic Skills of Young Adults. The Basic Skills Unit, ALBSU, 1994.

27  The Economist, 13/2/1993, "The M-word again".

28  Barzini, Luigi. The Europeans. London: Penguin, 1983.

29  Sampson, Anthony. The Essential Anatomy of Britain: Democracy in Crisis. London: Hodder & Stoughton, 1992.

30  The Economist, 2/10/1993, "The immortal remains of Margaret Thatcher".

31  Gallup for Europa Times, September 1993.

32  Malik, Rex. What's Wrong with British Industry?. London: Penguin, 1964.

33  International Management, September 1992, "Bottom of the Big League".

34  The Economist, 21/8/1993, "The Britain Audit: manufacturing".

35  International Herald Tribune, 23/2/1994, "A British National Humiliation, Quick Cash, Scarcely a Murmur".

36  Coopers & Lybrand, Made in the UK: The Middle Market Survey, 1994.

37  Financial Times, 13/4/1994, "Does nationality really matter?".

38  Coates, David. The Question of UK Decline. Hemel Hempstead: Harvester Wheatsheaf, 1994.

39  Horovitz, Jacques. Top Management Control in Europe. London: Macmillan, 1980.

40  Kinsman, Francis. Millenium: Towards Tomorrow's Society. London: Penguin, 1990.

41  Council for the Protection of Rural England, The Regional Lost Land, July 1993.

42  Bryson, Bill. Neither Here Nor There. London: Minerva, 1991.

43  Bellini, James. Rule Britannia. London: Abacus/Sphere Books, 1981.

44  Orwell, George. The Lion and the Unicorn. London, Penguin, 1982.

45  The Economist, 6/6/1992, "The people problem".

46  The Economist, 7/5/1994, "Local difficulties".

47   ICM Research, for The Observer, December 1993.

48   New Economics Foundation, Measuring Sustainable Economic Walfare, May 1994.

49   The Economist, 2/4/1994, "This is no way to clinch a deal".

# About the Author

A recognised lecturer and consultant in many countries of Europe, Richard Hill has had a lifetime of experience in international communications and cross-cultural relations. He has lived for long periods of time in the UK, Belgium, Austria, Spain and Switzerland, and has travelled widely. He speaks English, French, German and Spanish, with a 'dash' of Italian and Dutch.

His first book *"WeEuropeans"*, an examination of the mindsets, temperaments and value systems of the peoples of Europe was a non-fiction bestseller in a number of European markets and has been selected as course material by universities in Belgium, Finland, France, Germany, the Netherlands, and the United States.

A second book, "EuroManagers & Martians", looks at the business cultures of Europe and their inter-relationships, and is on the way to becoming a management reference book.

A popular speaker, Richard Hill maintains a heavy schedule of public engagements on the impact of cultural diversity. He was born in Leeds, England, and graduated with honours from Cambridge University in Economics and Modern Languages.

# WeEuropeans

Whatever doubts we may have about Maastricht, many of us hold fervently to the idea of a united Europe. And opinion polls among the young show a growing commitment to the European ideal.

This Europe is all about people – people who differ in their tastes and habits but share the same values and ideals. Understanding them, understanding one another, is a crucial step in the process of creating a Europe where unity cohabits with diversity.

Richard Hill talks about the people in this book. He starts by describing, then attacking, the stereotypes and moves on to a witty and skilful analysis of each of the European cultures.

He then enlarges his theme with a comparative analysis of value systems and lifestyles, how people communicate, relate to one another and do business. The final chapter examines recent events and offers thoughts on where we go from here.

*"...a fascinating book. His dissection of each nationality produces some wonderful sociological insights."*
**The European**

*"Richard Hill starts from the obvious to discover the difficult and makes an impressive success of it."*
**Emanuele Gazzo,** *Agence Europe*

*"A delightful and very funny book. I'll buy it!"*
**Derek Jameson,** *BBC Radio 2*

*"I can warmly recommend a wonderful book by Richard Hill, 'WeEuropeans'."* **Libby Purves,** *BA High Life*

# Have You Heard This One? An Anthology of European Jokes

**An Anthology of European Jokes**
in ENGLISH · in het NEDERLANDS · en FRANÇAIS · in DEUTSCH

Here are some of the better jokes we Europeans tell about one another. There are a lot of bad ones – far too many – but you will find none of them here.

Good European jokes are neither stupid nor abusive. They tell one something instructive about the way people from different cultures perceive one another. And some of these jokes shed light on the cultures of both the 'sender' and the 'receiver'.

Humour is the subtlest expression of culture, which explains why English people have difficulty in understanding German jokes. Even the psychology of humour is coloured by the attitudes of the different cultures. Yet there is common ground in European humour: some of these jokes turn up in various guises in various places.

As that eminent European Johann Wolfgang von Goethe said, rather severely: "There is nothing in which people more betray their character than in what they laugh at". Taken in the right spirit, humour is an excellent starting point for cross-cultural comprehension.

# EuroManagers & Martians

**EuroManagers & Martians**
Richard Hill

*The Business Cultures of Europe's Trading Nations*

Looking at them simply as people, when we see them in the streets of Paris or when we visit them *chez eux*, our fellow-Europeans come across as a pretty odd lot – a far cry from the Single Market, harmonisation and all those dreary things.

But how do they behave in business? Put a German, a Frenchman, a Spaniard, an Italian, a Swede and, of course, a Brit together around a negotiating table and what happens? Either nothing at all – they just don't know how to deal with one another – or a lot! It's then that you realise that, despite all the constraints of working within a business environment, life à *l'européenne* is still full of surprises.

The simple fact, of course, is that it would need a superhuman to leave his cultural baggage behind him simply because he puts on his coat to go to the office. This book examines the business cultures of Europe's main trading nations and offers useful insights into differences in attitudes to time, hierarchy, protocol, negotiating styles, acceptance of management disciplines and multicultural teamwork.

With so much cultural diversity even in business, the author wonders how on earth  we are going to develop the Euromanager we keep hearing about, the person who is going to save us from the Japanese, the Asian Tigers and others. Will this Euro-superman-ager ever exist?

*"The book is written from an alien's point of view, and it presents both carefully researched and anecdotal evidence in an entertaining read... Carefully steering a course away from the stereotype path, Hill gives well-considered and practical advice on conducting Eurobusiness."* **The European**

# What the press says

## International

*"...a fascinating book. His dissection of each nationality produces some wonderful sociological insights"*

**The European**

*"Richard Hill starts from the obvious to discover the difficult and makes an impressive success of it"*

**Emanuele Gazzo,** *Agence Europe*

*"For a thorough, fundamental understanding of what makes the neighbouring natives tick, this book is a must. Vive la différence!*

**Eurodiagnostic**

*"'**We**Europeans' is a lucid, readable book which achieves that most remarkable balance: it is serious and entertaining at the same time. It contains enough hard facts, anecdotes, and examples to make its analyses persuasive. Yet never does it bog down. It is 'must' reading for anyone who seeks to work or live transnationally - and intelligently - within the Europe of the late 20th century"*

**Andres Garrigo,** *Europe Today*

*"C'est un livre qui parle, j'allais dire avec tendresse, des Européens"*   **Serge Flamé,** *RTBF TV Belgium/TV5 Europe*

## Great Britain

*"A delightful and very funny book. I'll buy it!"*

**Derek Jameson,** *BBC Radio 2*

*"I can warmly recommend a wonderful book by Richard Hill, "**We**Europeans"*   *BA High Life*

*"A very European book, which I liked very much"*

*Manchester Evening News*

*"A new book called "WeEuropeans" explores the differences, but also celebrates what we have in common"*

*BBC Radio Scotland*

*"... a book that has been described as both serious and entertaining, and a 'must' for reading for anyone who seeks to work or live transnationally. And best of all, in my mind at least, it's got humour"* **Diana Luke,** *GLR Radio, London*

*"Let me commend to you his book called "WeEuropeans"... it's a fascinating read. He'll make you smile on page after page after page"* **Alex Dickson,** *Radio Clyde*

*"A good recipe for entertaining reading... for the pleasure of us all"* *Local Government Review*

## France

*"Cet ouvrage très documenté propose non sans humour, au-delà des stéréotypes habituels, une analyse pertinente et percutante"* *La Gazette du Tourisme*

*"One of the most interesting books I've ever looked at"* **Patrick Middleton,** *Riviera Radio*

*"An important and needed book has been published analyzing the welter of national mentalities that comprise the Old Continent. Entitled WeEuropeans, the book is already causing wide comment and discussion"* **John Van Den Bos,** *FUSAC*

## Germany

*"Das Buch 'Wir Europäer' des Engländers Richard Hill ist in Brüssel zum absoluten Bestseller avanciert. Mild ironisch analysiert er die Gewohnheiten der Euro-Völker, deckt Gemeinsamkeiten und Unterschiede auf, weist auf Stärken und Schwächen hin"* **Birgit Svensson,** *Wochenpost*

*"Wir Europäer: Zum Lachen!"* *BZ am Sonntag*

## Netherlands

*"'WeEuropeans' hoort verplichte lectuur te zijn voor elke deelnemer aan een Eurotop. Het zou de sfeer opvrolijken en de besluitvorming versnellen. De Europeanen, binnen en buiten de EG, zouden*

*er wel bij varen. Om hen gaat het toch altijd, beweren de regering-sleiders onvermoeid"*

**Henk Aben,** *Algemeen Dagblad*

*"Een onderhoudend boek, dat gezien de huidige ontwikkelingen binnen de Gemeenschap niet alleen actueel, maar ook leerzaam is"*

**Haye Thomas,** *Haagsche Courant*

*"Menselijke kijk op Europa"*      *Het Financiëele Dagblad*

*"Hill wil afrekenen met de bestaande, onjuiste stereotypen en - voor-al - streeft hij naar meer onderling begrip bij de volken binnen het Europese huis. Daarbij is hij niet over één nacht ijs gegaan. Tijdens zijn reizen heeft Hill allerlei eigenaardigheden en gebruiken van de Europese volken opgespoord. Zo is hij gekomen tot grappige constateringen"*     *Reformatorisch Dagblad*

# Luxembourg

*"Ainsi, il détruit bon nombre de mythes et révèle la richesse et la diversité de ce monde qui fait l'Europe"*     *Tageblatt*

*"Ein insgesamt sehr unterhaltsamer, nicht ganz bierernst zu neh-mender Beitrag zum Dauerthema 'Europa' - wohltuend besonders durch den Verzicht auf jegliche 'ethnocentricity' und den stets mit-schwingenden humoristischen Unterton"*     *Letzeburger Journal*

*"Un livre très amusant, rédigé en anglais par un "British man in Brussels"*     *Euromagazine*

# Belgium

*"Richard Hill, een in België wonende Brit, ging in zijn boek 'WeEuropeans' op zoek naar het hoe en waarom van dat tegenstrij-dige Europa, naar de kloof tussen wil en daad, utopie en realiteit. Hij stuitte daarbij op vaak diepgewortelde nationale en regionale reflexen"*

*De Standaard Magazine*

*"Nous allons parler aujourd'hui d'un livre qui n'est pas écrit en français, mais en anglais, un anglais assez facile d'accès d'ailleurs pour tous ceux qui connaissent cette langue, et d'ailleurs pour ceux qui l'étudient c'est un excellent exercice"*   **Jean-Paul Andret,** *RTL TV*

*"De britse premier Thatcher zei ooit dat als de Europese éénwording doorgaat zoals ze bezig is alle nationale eigenschappen zullen verdwijnen en er een soort Europese éénheidsmens zal ontstaan. Onzin, vindt Hill"* **Guy Janssen**, *BRT1 TV*

*"Ich bin der Meinung, dass dieses Werk für Supra-National-Denkende und Supra-National-Agierende ein Muss sein sollte, analysiert es doch messerscharf sogennante Stereotypen. Mit viel Humanismus, Witz, Liebe zum Detail, Zärtlichkeit und Fachkenntnis zeigt Richard Hill uns auf gleichzeitig ernste und unterhaltsame aber auch auf überzeugende und intelligente Weise, wo die Wurzel unserer Heimat sich befindet: nämlich in einer europäischen Identität der Gleichheit in der Verschiedenheit"* **Helmuth Hilgers**, *BRF Radio*

*"Richard Hill est anglais et pourtant il adore l'Europe... L'Europe pour lui ce n'est ni le PAC, ni la DGIII ni le paquet Delors ni même la D2 MacPacket... mais des gens, des habitudes, des tics, des différences. Une richesse formidable qui donne plutôt l'envie de rire que de pleurer ou de manifester devant le Berlaymont d'ailleurs vide. Richard Hill sait capter l'air du temps... c'est drôle, mouvementé, documenté..."* **Myriam Gooris**, *Radio 21*

*"Il fallait être Britannique pour oser le pari, il fallait avoir vécu longtemps à Bruxelles pour le réussir. C'est le cas de l'Anglais Richard Hill"* **Violaine Muûls**, *L'Evénement*

*"'WeEuropeans' is an excellent read on many levels, whether for the expert who is looking for new ideas to research or for those who are looking to understand their neighbours (and themselves) a little better"* *AmCham*

*"Même lorsqu'il égratigne légèrement l'une ou l'autre susceptibilité nationale, l'auteur ne le fait jamais méchamment car il se veut compréhensif, non dénué de tendresse et d'humour qui vous feront sourire lorsque vous vous reconnaîtrez au travers de la lecture"* *Swissnews*

*"In his book Richard Hill addresses the differences... he says that they have reasons for existing, he just had to figure out what they were"* *Radio Flanders International*

*"From health to hygiene, humour to holidays, Hill leaves no stereo-type unturned"* The Bulletin

*"'WeEuropeans' will entertain even the best-travelled European. For those whose experience is limited to only one or two countries, it comes under the heading of essential reading"* Business Journal

*"This is a book about Europeans - a description of characteristics, attitudes, hopes and habits along the continent's ethnic and national divides. More than a simple country-by-country profile of personality and prejudice, Mr Hill has attempted to root in their history and culture much of how Europeans appear to others"* Business Links

*"Ik wens u veel plezier toe met uw boek "WeEuropeans", veel succes"* **Tony Van den Bosch**, BRT TV, De Zevende Dag

# The Nordic Countries

*"Mens velgere i stadig flere land vender seg mot sine ledere og deres store unions-dremmer; hva er mer aktuelt enn en bok som vil ta oss med på en kulturell reise i det europeiske mangfold?"* Dagbladet, Norway

*"Godt er det, for Norge og nordmenn har fått en relativt mild og hederlig omtale, sammenlignet med de andre europeiske land og folk"* Aftonbladet, Norway

*"Det fastslår den britiske markedsføreren og PR-mannen Richard Hill, nå ute på det norske bokmarkedet med den internasjonale best-seller 'Vi europeere'. En bok om folk og kulturer i vår mangfoldige verdensdel"* Kampanje, Norway

*"I bästsäljaren 'We Europeans' finns vi redan med på ett hörn, som ett hyggligt men gammaldags folk med dörrar som öppnas utåt... 'We Europeans', en munter och innehållsrik bok som snabbt blivit populär bland EG-folket"* Dagens Nyheter, Sweden

*"Hill mainitsee sivumennen myös, että suomalaiset juovat paljon. Tämäkin mielikuvaongelma jälleen kerran! Lukiessa eteenpäin käy ilmi, että hän tarkoittaa maidon kulutusta"* Turun Sanomat, Finland

# Services Available

Europublic represents the author of this book, Richard Hill, a consultant specialising in cross-cultural relations and communications, and the impact of cultures on business styles.

In addition to book publishing, Europublic provides speakers on cross-cultural topics and conducts tailored in-company training courses on cultural issues impacting on organisations operating in an international and multicultural environment.

Richard Hill is a regular speaker at international conferences, business seminars and congresses. His clients include institutes of management, business schools, universities, trade federations and private-sector companies, amongst others the EuroChannels organisation, GE Capital, Honeywell, IBM International Education Centre, Lowe International, Medtronic and 3Com Europe.

He also lectures at universities and management schools in the UK, Belgium, the Netherlands, Germany, Sweden and Finland.

**For further information on these services, please mail or fax to:**

**Karin Minke**
**Europublic SA/NV**
**Avenue W. Churchill 11 ( box 21 )**
**B-1180 Brussels**
**Tel.: +32-2-343.77.26**
**Fax: +32-2-343.93.30**

O **Great Britain, Little England**
ISBN 74-4440-04-5    BF 495   £ 9.99   DM 29.90   HFL 25.-   SFR 24.90

O **WeEuropeans**
ISBN 90-74440-01-0   BF 640   £12.99   DM 39.90   HFL 35.-   SFR 29.90

O **EuroManagers & Martians**
ISBN 90-74440-02-9   BF 695   £12.99   DM 39.90   HFL 38.50  SFR 29.90

O **Have You Heard This One?**
**An Anthology of European Jokes**
ISBN 90-74440-03-7   BF 195   £ 3.99   DM 12.90   HFL 9.95   SFR 6.95

These books are distributed throughout Europe.

If you have difficulty in obtaining any of these books through your local bookstore, you can order through the publisher:

**Europublic SA / NV,**
**Avenue Winston Churchill 11 (box 21), B-1180 Brussels**
**Tel. +32-2-343.77.26 - Fax +32-2-343.93.30**

Name: ...............................................................................

Address:..........................................................................

.......................................................................................

.......................................................................................

Tel: ....................................... Fax: ...................................